A Guide for Students and Graduates
or Anyone Making a Fresh Start

AJ,

HERE YOU GO! HOPE YOU

LIKE IT,

DON'T F***
THIS UP!

How To Get What You Want In Life

FRED STUVEK JR.

Don't F*** This Up!

For information about this title or to order other books and/or electronic media, contact the publisher:
Triumvirate Press
617 W. Main Street
Knoxville, Tennessee 37902
TriumviratePress@gmail.com itstartswithyou.net

ISBNs: 978-1-7323060-4-2 (softcover)
        978-1-7323060-5-9 (ePub)
        978-1-7323060-6-6 (Kindle)

Printed in the United States of America

Cover and Interior design: 1106 Design
Publisher's Cataloging-In-Publication Data
(Prepared by The Donohue Group, Inc.)

Names: Stuvek, Fred, Jr., author.

Title: Don't f*** this up! : how to get what you want in life / Fred Stuvek, Jr.

Other Titles: Don't fuck this up!

Description: Knoxville, Tennessee : Triumvirate Press, [2020] | "A graduate's guide."

Identifiers: ISBN 9781732306042 (softcover) | ISBN 9781732306059 (ePub) | ISBN 9781732306066 (Kindle)

Subjects: LCSH: Young adults--Life skills guides. | Young adults--Conduct of life. | Success.

Classification: LCC HQ799.5 S78 2020 (print) | LCC HQ799.5 (ebook) | DDC 646.700842--dc23

Contents

Preface

Whether you are a soon-to-be graduate from high school or college, or a recent graduate seeking to enter the workforce, your world is about to change. You have some important decisions to make. These decisions will chart your course as you set off on your journey of learning and self-discovery. Depending on your decisions and your desires, you are about to transition from either one learning institution to another or from an institution to a company or professional field. Many people struggle when making these transitions, finding themselves ill-prepared, with gaps in the skills and abilities required for success. Moreover, many hold unrealistic expectations, which, combined with unpreparedness, result in a host of problems that severely compromise one's ability to be successful and fulfilled.

When faced with these issues, you have questions, concerns, even fear about what to do next. You need help, but you are not sure where to go, who to ask, or even what questions to ask. As you struggle to find answers and direction, you make decisions that you believe are in your best interest. But if you aren't asking the right questions, then you aren't getting the right answers. This process will not get you to where you need to be.

As you anguish about the uncertainty of your decisions, rest assured, you are by no means alone in this regard. The issues you face are not insurmountable or out of your control. There is a process that will help you through this, and you should take solace in the fact that, by taking the initiative to read this book, you've given yourself an invaluable tool that will aid you in finding the right path, making the right decisions, and achieving your desired outcome.

I am fortunate to have been exposed to myriad experiences that have enabled me to learn, grow, and achieve success. My experience covers a fairly broad range, one which I have been told is unique—although it never occurred to me until someone mentioned it. I have a sports background, having competed at the highest levels at an intercollegiate level. I have a military background by virtue of my education and training at the United States Naval Academy and subsequent military service. I have a business background in both the private and public sector, and I started up and sold my own company. Over the course of my career, I've learned many lessons and adopted various principles and best practices that served me well. These principles apply to whatever you want to do with your life and career. They are proven; they work, and they get results.

The principles that I will describe are fundamental, essential, and never changing. They are timeless and recession-proof. Whether in ancient Greece, London, Kyoto, Peking, or colonial Boston, these same principles were seen as the basic underpinnings of success. If your fundamentals are sound, you can build on them, and you will more effectively understand and deal with complexities. This foundation will serve as a safeguard when addressing the opportunities, challenges, and adversity you will face over the course of your chosen career.

You will notice throughout this book principles and recommendations related to both your professional and personal life. This is because behavior and success or failure in one area inevitably spills into another, which is why I use the term "balance" several times.

This book is written in such a way that each chapter builds on the previous one in a comprehensive, yet focused, manner. Explanations are given as to why each principle is important, with instructions on how to improve in each area as skills are learned and developed. Adhering to this regimen gives you the opportunity to unlock your potential by changing your mindset, putting you in an action mode that will allow you to attain your goals and achieve success, fulfillment, and happiness.

Throughout this book, the terms "belief" and "mindset" are used frequently. Your achievement in life will be determined largely by your mindset, or the belief and confidence you have in yourself and what you do. You will never reach your true potential without this steadfast belief and confidence. A person who believes in himself or herself cannot be defeated. Their belief makes them strong. They have a warrior-like mindset, they have the will to prevail, and they have trained themselves to be the best.

As you read and contemplate your next steps, remember that life is about decisions. The life you will live is the life you will have created, based on the decisions you make and the habits you form. This book will highlight the issues you will face, the habits that you will form, and the process necessary for you to make the very best decisions for you and your future. I will provide you with the instructions you'll require, as well as motivation during this process and beyond as you embark on your journey.

PART ONE

Find Something You Believe In, and Get Good at It

"You owe it to yourself to understand what motivates you, and match those beliefs with your personality, skill set, interests, and values. Only then will you be able to optimize your prospects for success, fulfillment, and happiness."

—Fred Stuvek Jr.

CHAPTER ONE

Believe

"If you believe it will work out, you will see opportunities.
If you believe it won't, you will see obstacles."

—Wayne Dyer

The single most important quality for achieving any degree of success and happiness is belief. This simple word is one of the most powerful words in our vocabulary. It is the central force behind success, and it is the key trait found in every accomplished person. If you do not believe in yourself, how do you expect someone else to believe in you? Without belief, you will never realize your full potential.

There is something you can do to unleash the ultimate potential that resides within each and every one of us. It is a process that takes time. It requires a plan, along with the commitment and discipline to follow through. The sooner you commit, the quicker you will realize your full potential. There are two essential parts to believing: the first is belief in yourself; the second is belief in what you are doing. You may have the first without the second, or vice versa, but if one of these is missing, you have a mismatch. When both are present, however, the combination is formidable and will enable you to realize your ultimate potential. This is your goal.

We all start with dreams and goals. We imagine being successful, happy, and fulfilled. Sometimes—perhaps many times—things don't go the way we thought they would. We have setbacks, which we view as failures. As these accumulate, we start to doubt ourselves. We find ourselves stuck in a rut and feel trapped. We focus too much on what went wrong, crediting setbacks to factors beyond our control. We feel ineffective, sometimes giving up and retreating to whatever safe haven we can. We continue in a mode of behavior that reinforces this downward trend. We realize life can be tough and unfair, and we become disillusioned. We lose confidence in ourselves and our abilities, sinking to the point where we cease believing in ourselves. We have feelings of helplessness and despair, possibly affecting even our health. And unless we change, nothing will change as we continue this treadmill of failure. Does any of this sound familiar? Perhaps you know someone who is trapped in this cycle. You may have even found yourself in a similar situation by this point in your life. We need to break the cycle or, better yet, keep it from starting altogether. Otherwise every day will be the same, like it was for Bill Murray in *Groundhog Day*.

You have undoubtedly heard that "you have to believe in yourself" several times. But has anyone ever sat down with you and explained what you need to do to believe in yourself? Have you ever seen a description or a plan? You probably haven't. However, there is a plan you can follow to get to a point in life where you believe in yourself and have a greater sense of purpose. It will require not one action, but myriad steps to effect this transformation. And there is only one person who can make it happen—you.

The first thing to do is to get your mind right, especially your subconscious. It tells you what you are already inclined or disinclined to do. For example, how many times have you approached something with the attitude "I don't think this is a good idea" or "I don't think this is going to work out"? And what happened? In nearly every instance, it didn't work out because you did not believe it could. You were conditioning yourself for failure at the outset. Conversely, how many times have you approached something with the attitude "I can do this" or "I've got this"? What happened? In nearly every instance, it did work out, because you believed it could and conditioned yourself for success.

The mind can be trained and conditioned, just like any other muscle in your body. If you train and condition your mind properly, your prospects for success increase exponentially. The right mindset enables you to create and develop tactics for success. This can-do attitude is infectious and rubs off on those around you, just as a negative or defeatist attitude can be poisonous to others.

Individuals who foster a positive attitude tend to live happier lives than those who constantly expect doom and gloom. This is a key component for success and quality of life. Numerous studies have highlighted the impact a positive attitude has on your success, happiness, and health.

Having a positive attitude will also help you in your interaction with others. Your attitude will resonate. You will give off a positive vibe, and people will gravitate toward you. They will invest their time with someone who has a mindset that gets things done, not with someone who is constantly negative and focusing on why something can't be done.

A positive mindset is not something that is achieved by chance, nor is a person genetically hardwired to have a positive mindset. It is something that you make manifest, and it is shaped by the learning experiences that mold you into the person you'll ultimately become. These accumulating experiences and accomplishments condition you, driving the development of skills and proficiencies needed to achieve your goals. Some of these skills involve formal training or education, some of them are life- or business-related, and others are informal, small lessons learned over time. Regardless of the process, first you need to have a plan with goals and follow-through, without which you will simply drift from one harbor to the next without direction. The importance of a plan—and your willingness and ability to persevere and follow through—is the basic premise of this book.

Working in tandem with belief in oneself and a positive attitude, an unyielding sense of purpose is the driving force in your life and your future career. It is the burning belief in what you are doing that determines the difference between success and failure. History is replete with examples.

The Revolutionary War—the American colonies' fight for independence from England—is a good example. If one were to take an objective look, prior to victory, at the chances of the colonies winning their independence in a war against arguably the single most powerful country on Earth at the time, you would have to admit that the prospects were dim, at best. In Paul Kennedy's book *The Rise and Fall of the Great Powers,* he makes a more-than-convincing case that the strength of a nation is best measured by its industrial power or capacity relative to other nations. He uses such factors as population, urbanization, per-capita levels of iron and steel production, energy consumption, and other factors to calculate an industrialization rate. In the eighteenth century, the American colonies' industrialization index was a small fraction of England's. Based on these data, the colonies should have never won the war. In retrospect, it is one of the few times in history that a country with such a disparity in industrial resources was able to achieve victory. Granted, there were some other mitigating factors, most notably command-and-control problems for the British, exacerbated by distance and slow communication, but one must admit that the American colonies' prospects for victory and freedom must not have been very encouraging.

However, the founding fathers had a resolute and steadfast belief in their cause, even at their own peril. Look at what happened to many of those fifty-six individuals who signed the Declaration of Independence, knowing full well the penalty would be death if they were captured. Many lost their homesteads, their property, and even their lives. How many of us today would have that same conviction? Would you?

"Quo Vadis?" is a Latin phrase meaning, "Where are you going?" This phrase is used figuratively to describe someone seeking a career path.

Deciding what you want to do with your life is not revolutionary—it is evolutionary. It determines, in many cases, where you go to school, what type of training you receive, what type of job you take, where you might live, and your income potential. You will spend a great deal of time endeavoring to determine what defines and shapes you as a person.

When deciding on a major in college or a career path, ask yourself, "Why?" Why are you picking this major, this career path? Is it something you believe in and enjoy doing? Or is it simply because the money is good? While money is important—because everyone has bills to pay—money alone is not a strategy for success and happiness. It is your underlying belief and sense of purpose that set the stage for success. If this passion is lacking, it will ultimately catch up with you. It will manifest itself in your attitude, performance, and stress level, and may even affect your health as you suffer the drudgery of doing something you do not have passion for simply because the money is good.

When making a career choice, take time to take a personal inventory. What is it that you like to do and feel passionate about? There is an adage, "Find something you enjoy doing and would do for free—that is what you should be doing." While this may seem like an oversimplification, it is love for what you do that enables you to deal with the adversity that lies ahead.

What are your strengths and weaknesses relative to what you want to do? Do you believe you can get better? How do you capitalize on your strengths and overcome what you see as weaknesses? Do you need further schooling or training? What do you need to do to make it happen? It is useful to get input from others. Ask your parents, your teachers, and your friends what they see as your chief attributes. Sometimes we see ourselves one way, and others see us another; your real self is probably somewhere in between. Soliciting input from others gives you a different perspective, raises points never considered, and provides deeper insight and new ideas. Be open to input. Don't be defensive. Listen.

Spend some time on yourself, and continue to move forward, learn, and grow. With time and experience, the answer will come if you are listening. In former times, it was more common for someone to merely get a general degree and decide what they wanted to do after they'd entered the workforce, initially following no career path in particular. In today's global environment, which is more transparent and competitive, there are greater demands and requirements for specific skill sets, rewarding focus and specialization. Be proactive; seek out as much experience as possible to broaden your knowledge to help you home in on what is the best fit for you, and then follow that path.

Chinese general and philosopher Sun Tzu summed it up best two thousand years ago, when he stated, "You have to believe in yourself." The veracity of this statement cannot be refuted. If you believe, you will achieve, but first you must:

1. *Believe:* In yourself—this is where it starts.

2. *Believe:* In what you are doing.

3. *Find:* Identify a good fit for you.

4. *Plan:* Develop a plan.

5. *Act:* Commit, execute, and follow through.

CHAPTER TWO

Fit

"Let your past guide you, not decide you."

A recent study indicated that half of U.S. workers are unhappy in their current job. The primary reason is bad fit, which is what happens when a job does not match up with someone's personality, skill set, or interests, or when the company culture is inconsistent with an individual's core values. This mismatch causes anxiety and stress, resulting in disillusionment and disengagement. If neither the career nor the company is a good fit, it is the worst of both worlds.

You will spend much of your life at work. You owe it to yourself to understand what inspires and motivates you, and to match those beliefs with your personality, skill set, interests, and values, since only then will you be able to optimize your prospects for success, fulfillment, and happiness.

Deciding on a career is part art and part science. It is an art because it is personal. It is a science because it is a five-step process requiring assessment, investigation, alignment, career choice, and company choice. Combining the science and art will point you in the right direction.

Assess

"Know thyself," the Greek philosopher Socrates stated. This principle particularly applies when choosing a career path, as the better you know yourself, the greater your chances are of finding the right fit.

Self-assessment requires introspection and an objective look at yourself. Not being objective, not being honest with yourself can develop into an avoidance trap, which can subsequently lead you in the wrong direction—or nowhere at all. Conducting a self-assessment enhances your ability to identify your interests, skills, personality, and values. *Interests* are what you enjoy doing. *Skills* are abilities you acquire or what you do best. *Personality* is the set of characteristics that determines your behavior. *Values* are what is important to you.

Ask yourself, "What do I enjoy doing? Where have I excelled?" The answer lies in recognizing those activities you find interesting, satisfying, and stimulating. Conversely, admitting what you do not enjoy strengthens and balances your assessment process. Do not take lightly the statement, "We are best when we are doing what we enjoy most." Too often, this observation is ignored or underestimated. It is an important factor for career choice and satisfaction, and will keep you engaged and motivated throughout your career.

Analyze your skills and how they fit your interests. Your skill set is a combination of factors contributing to your ability to perform a certain task or accomplish a specific goal. Your skill set can be broken down into three categories. The first category is skills you have acquired through either education or past work experience; these are referred to as "technical" or "hard" skills. The second category is skills that reflect your personality and behavior, referred to as "soft" skills. The third category is "transferable" skills, which are skills that you can take with you wherever you go. Soft skills are transferable, whereas technical skills may or may not be transferable to your job, since they are specific.

Personality plays an important role in your success and affects your professional performance, personal life, and overall success. Understanding your personality and choosing a career that fits you improve your prospects for performance and job satisfaction. There are various methods to assess personality traits, for example, the Meyers-Briggs personality assessment and other similar online tools. Solicit input from high school or college career counselors, and take advantage of feedback from those closest to you as they observe you in various situations. They can provide input on their perception of your strengths and weaknesses.

Values are beliefs and ideas that are important to you. Your choice of a career and a specific company should mesh with your values. Values such as selflessness, honesty, and integrity are intrinsic values or core beliefs. Values such as wealth, position, and title are extrinsic values and byproducts of your work. Determining your values and aligning them with your career are important. A mismatch of personal values and employment is one of the greatest sources of frustration in the workplace, as you end up having to constantly compromise, which can potentially spill over into your personal life.

Investigate

Investigate and explore your specific areas of interest once you have taken a personal assessment. Research sources include the web, books, journals, career fairs, and industry professionals. Take career-specific tests as necessary to further identify targeted professions. Join various clubs, do volunteer work, or get a summer job.

While in college, research your degree. Look at careers others have pursued, and talk with graduates to learn the pros and cons of the profession. Internships can be valuable firsthand experience, as it is difficult to know if you are going to like something if you have never done it. If internships are not available, take the initiative and make contact with companies, and ask to meet with or shadow individuals who are in your targeted profession.

Keep an open mind, and don't hesitate to consider opportunities to explore other options. In high school, I went on a number of recruiting trips to colleges and universities, but I wasn't convinced any of them were a good fit. That changed in March of my senior year, when I was contacted by the Naval Academy and was urged to make a visit. The thought of going there had never crossed my mind. However, I had never been to Annapolis, so I kept an open mind and agreed to visit. Upon arrival, I noticed that a schedule of meetings had been arranged with not only football coaches but also company officers, professors, and midshipmen, in addition to an extensive tour of the campus. Discussions focused on what would be required, the training involved, and what commitments would be necessary. Topics such as duty, honor, and discipline were stressed. I took everything in, reflected that evening, and realized everything I'd heard that day were values and principles I believed in. I knew I belonged there. I felt that the training and education would help me develop in many ways and make me a better person. The next day, before leaving for home, I said, "I'm in. Tell me what I need to do." In hindsight, keeping an open mind and taking the opportunity to explore this option resulted in one of the best decisions in my life.

As you go through this process, don't be nearsighted. You may think one way but end up going another. There are career choices out there today that did not exist a year ago. Do not be beholden to conventional choices. Think outside the box, and explore multiple options.

Align

Knowing yourself, understanding your strengths and weaknesses, and aligning them with your career choice and work environment add up to a win, for both you and the company. Studies have shown that matching a career with your interests and personality results in greater satisfaction and fulfillment. Individuals who are successful, fulfilled, and happy in their careers are motivated and energized when they go to work. They look at their job as a venue in which they can apply their talent and skills, and as a place where they find more meaning and purpose, with less stress and better health. "Alignment" refers to balance. Lack of balance between your personal values and your work environment can lead to a lack of motivation. No matter how good the money, if your work is not meaningful and rewarding, you will lack the motivation and passion necessary to sustain yourself day in and day out throughout your career, to weather challenges and adversity, and to achieve great success.

Consider both your personal and work values as you contemplate various careers. As mentioned earlier, a mismatch in values is a formula for conflict. Pursuing a career path that matches your values will result in a more fulfilled life, as work helps determine your self-image and self-worth. While there may have to be trade-offs, it's a two-way street: ensure that the right balance is struck, concentrating on those values and aspects of your work that deliver the greatest satisfaction. Once you have decided, the next step is to pursue your career choice.

Develop

Develop a career plan together with a communication and networking plan, including short- and long-term goals, with specific actions. Do not underestimate the importance of the résumé. It should differentiate you by conveying those traits that make you a unique candidate for their organization. If you require assistance with your résumé, engage the services of a professional.

Sending out dozens of unsolicited résumés each week via the Internet can give one a false sense of accomplishment; it is not the most effective way to find an opportunity. The most effective method is networking via established contacts, existing professional organizations, and forums used for recruitment. LinkedIn is a good example: 87 percent of all employers use

LinkedIn as a recruitment tool. Employment agencies are also an option for industry-specific opportunities. Do not sit back and wait for something to happen. Take the initiative, and do not be afraid to cold-call.

Geographic considerations are important when making career-choice decisions. A larger, urban environment will present more options, with specific industries located in certain hubs. Having the flexibility to relocate provides additional choices, with the further benefits of making more personal connections and enhancing your ability to network, which could bear fruit in the future.

Lifestyles and priorities change over the course of your career. Ideally, by the time you are in your mid-thirties to early forties, you will have found your stride and can focus on job enrichment, increased proficiency, and further opportunities within your chosen field, striking a balance with your personal life. If you ever find yourself disillusioned or dissatisfied, that does not mean you cannot make a change. Regardless of what stage of your career you find yourself in down the road, it is always possible to reassess and explore other opportunities utilizing the steps outlined in this chapter.

Identify

A company's culture reflects their values, practices, and beliefs. Research to determine if the culture is a good fit for you, starting with the company's website. Look at the mission statement, the section that describes the company and why it was founded. Review recent articles or press releases. Research social media for employee and customer comments. When looking at some of the comments written by employees, former employees, or customers, bear in mind that not everything you read is true.

Look at the leadership team, and read their biographies, noting their education, work experience, and background. The leadership team determines the culture in mid- to smaller-size companies. For example, if a company is led by people with a military background, and you are a laid-back, type-B individual, it is conceivable that the company may not be a good fit.

Is the company large, small, established, or a start-up? There are pros and cons to each one. Your personality, goals, and what you are looking for in a company will determine the better fit for you. If you are a structured individual, want to focus on a specific area, and value a predictable career path with stability, a larger company may be a better match.

If you are more entrepreneurial and adventurous, consider a smaller company or even a start-up, especially if there is an opportunity for ownership. You will be exposed to and involved in more aspects of business than in a larger, more-structured environment. You may wear a number of different hats and will not be as shielded as you would be in a larger company. A smaller company will magnify what you do, both good and bad. In this environment, you will gain a better understanding and appreciation for the various aspects of business. You will learn to analyze and solve problems in a different way, since this environment often requires unconventional solutions, encouraging innovation and creativity.

Having worked all throughout the spectrum, my preference is a smaller, nimbler environment with an entrepreneurial flair. You may find it to be the case for you as well, but ensure that it is at the right time in your career. I chose to join a larger company upon entering the workforce after my military service. I was regimented and disciplined by virtue of my previous experience, and at that time, it was a good fit. This helped to lay the groundwork for me to transition to different business environments throughout my career.

Once you have done your research and selected potential companies, the next step is the interview. The interview is not only an opportunity for employers to assess you; it also allows you to assess your potential boss and colleagues to determine if the position would be a good fit. How your interviewers conduct themselves in your interview could be a window into what it would be like to work with and for them. Do they greet you with a smile and a firm handshake or remain seated behind the desk? Do they shut the door and give you their full attention? Do they listen to what you have to say, or do they do most of the talking? Do they talk mostly about themselves? Do they seem distracted, constantly checking their watch, phone, or email? If they don't give you time and attention during your interview, they will likely not give you time and respect when you work with them.

The same holds true when meeting with other managers and employees of the company. What is their demeanor? How would you classify the interactions with the people you meet? Are they friendly, energetic, and enthusiastic? When you ask questions, are the answers consistent, using positive terms to describe the company and their role in it? Is the visit properly organized? Even if it is a smaller company or a start-up, they should still be able to operate efficiently. Take note of the surroundings. Are there offices and cubicles, or is it more of an open workspace? What is the dress code?

What type of vibe do you get? What is your initial reaction to the possibility of working in such an environment? Position, salary, and benefits are important considerations; however, you need to consider how much time you'll be spending there. If it is a bad fit—if it is inconsistent with your personality, skills, interests, or values—you will not look forward to going to work, which will negatively affect your performance. If you have any doubts, your instinct is telling you something—listen to it, and continue with the process:

1. *Assess:* Identify your interests, skills, personality, and values. Know yourself.

2. *Investigate:* Research and explore your areas of interest. Keep an open mind.

3. *Align:* Determine which career fits you. Stay balanced.

4. *Develop:* Craft a career plan. Stay organized.

5. *Identify:* Determine which company is the best fit for you. If the shoe fits, wear it.

Goals

*"The fact that you aren't where you want to
be should be enough motivation."*

"If you don't know where you are going, any road will take you there" captures a famous exchange between Alice and the Cheshire Cat in Lewis Carroll's book, *Alice in Wonderland.* The same could be said of your career and your life: without a sense of purpose, you lack direction.

If you look at anyone who is successful, it wasn't by accident or serendipity. One of the common traits among successful individuals, in whatever walk of life, is goal setting. They have a vision, they set goals, and they take action. These goals give direction, a sense of purpose, and motivation.

A goal is a specific statement of an outcome that an individual or a company wants to achieve, usually within a specified time frame. Examples of personal goals are buying a house, losing weight, running a marathon, or becoming a CEO. Examples of business goals would be increasing market share, improving customer service, or being debt free. Goals are typically divided into a series of steps or concrete objectives. Companies and people sometimes don't understand the difference and use the terms "goals" and "objectives" interchangeably—and incorrectly. A goal is where you want to go. An objective is a measurable step required to achieve your goal.

As mentioned in the preceding chapter, the first course of action is to determine what you want to do, which should be something you believe in, enjoy doing, and can do well. Take the necessary time to consider your goals and your definition of "success." What would you see as a successful conclusion to what you are doing, in both the short and long terms?

Goal setting is important to bridge the gap between the mind and the body. Taking time to set goals creates a bias toward action and change, rather than continuing your daily routine on autopilot. Goal setting changes your mindset and keeps you from reverting to your default mode. The body follows the mind, and as you think about these goals, your physical side comes into play, putting you into action mode.

In this context, the Chinese proverb "The journey of a thousand miles begins with one step" is apropos. Getting something accomplished means taking that first step. Do not procrastinate and make excuses. Everything may seem the same today, but a year from now, many things will have changed, including potential opportunities. The sooner you start, the sooner you reach your goal, all the while positioning yourself to take advantage of opportunities that arise, since you are in a growth mindset.

Upon completing my military service, I entered the business world. After a few years, I concluded that my career aspirations would be bolstered if I received a Master of Business Administration degree, or an MBA. I did not want to find myself being considered for a position without having that box checked—I knew it would put me at a disadvantage someday. The catalyst was a meeting with some clients in the president's office, when, somehow, the conversation turned to graduate school. I was asked, "You have an MBA, don't you?" I hastily replied, "I do not, but I will have one in two years," followed by everyone nodding approvingly. After the meeting, I immediately drove to a university that had an MBA program, went to the admissions office, and told them I wanted to go to night school for the degree. They asked, "When do you want to start?" I told them "Immediately," even though they were already a couple of weeks into the semester. They remarked that it wasn't possible, as I had to first complete a lengthy application process. I took an application and filled it out on the spot, promising to get the rest of the documents to them quickly. I found a class of interest in the MBA program, and, the next night, I attended, despite the fact that I was not yet officially enrolled. I told the instructor my application was being processed, and I did not want to miss any more classes in the meantime. He was surprised, but let me sit in. I later purchased the textbook and caught up on the material I had missed. After a few weeks, administration relented, and I was admitted to the program. Two years later, I had the MBA.

As it turns out, a few years after that, I was being considered for a position in one of the subsidiaries of the company, and one of the requirements was a graduate degree. The box was checked. I was ultimately offered the position and accepted it, which turned out to be the right decision for a number of reasons. I have often wondered how things would have turned out if I had not had that MBA box checked.

Establish

When people think of goals, they are often inclined to focus solely on career goals, failing to address personal goals. Do not neglect your personal goals—they are just as important and are essential to maintaining balance. It is difficult to be fulfilled overall if one part of your life is flourishing and the other is not. Things have a way of spilling over.

Studies have demonstrated that individuals who set goals are more likely to be successful than those who do not. This applies to any aspect of your life. Setting goals for yourself triggers a psychological reaction that makes you action-oriented and more focused, putting you on course to success.

Setting goals is not a defined skill. You need to learn how to manage the process, ensuring that your goals are realistic. You must have a clear idea of what you want to achieve and what is needed to get there. Set both extrinsic and intrinsic goals in order to achieve the proper balance. You can very well achieve fame and fortune, but if you are not personally fulfilled and happy, it will not feel like true success.

Define

The acronym SMART is commonly used in conjunction with the goal-setting process. Each goal should be "**S**pecific, **M**easurable, **A**ttainable, **R**elevant, and **T**ime-related."

Goals should be substantive enough that the desired result is clear and understood. A personal goal of "getting in shape," while admirable, is too vague. You need more specific parameters. The same holds true with gaining market share, which is a professional goal, but once again, not specific enough. Conversely, a goal can be *too* specific if it does not efficiently contribute to the desired result, leading you in the wrong direction. These types of goals are often quantitative in nature, short-term oriented, and do not align with the long-term vision, resulting in wasted time and resources. This misalignment normally occurs in the corporate environment, where personal interests can sometimes override corporate goals, and is caused by improper goal setting and lack of oversight by management.

Prioritize

There is only so much time and so many resources available to accomplish your goals. Plan and prioritize based on what will have the biggest impact on what you want to achieve, efficiently budgeting your time, which is your most important resource. Having too many goals with no prioritization will get nothing done—or at least not done *well*.

Some of your goals will be short-term, and others will be long-term. Short-term goals are measured in days, weeks, and months—no longer than one year. Long-term goals are measured in years, two to three years out or even longer. The accomplishment of short-term goals should contribute to achieving long-term goals, and you need to strike a balance. Having only short-term goals does not give you a clear focus on what you want to achieve in the long term. The knowledge that your accomplishment of short-term goals is contributing to your long-term goals reinforces your behavior, maintains your momentum, and motivates you to keep moving forward.

As you prioritize your goals, consider impact and time. What will have the single biggest impact? How much time do you have? What is the timeline associated with attaining the goal? Just because you do not feel like doing something or don't enjoy doing it does not make it a lower priority if it is mission critical. By the same token, if you have two goals of equal importance and can't decide which to complete first, go with the one you are most confident in attaining. If some of the goals seem daunting, break them down into smaller, more manageable steps that, when successfully concluded, all contribute to attainment of the goal.

Document

Once you have identified and prioritized your goals, it is mandatory that you put them in writing. Formally documenting your goals provides clarity and avoids ambiguity. Studies have shown that individuals who put their goals in writing realize greater success than those who do not. Documentation also gives you a road map you can later refer to in order to refocus on where you are going and what you need to do to get there. The more aware you are of your goals and your progress, the more focused and less distracted you will be.

Share your goals with others, especially those who are close to you. They will have a better understanding and appreciation for what you are doing. Enlisting their support creates a further degree of accountability, as you do not want to be put in the position of having to offer excuses or explain away why something wasn't finished. This greater transparency provides further motivation, and you will be pleasantly surprised to find that others are supportive of your goals and provide valuable feedback.

There are various techniques that can reinforce your goals and keep them front and center. Notes in the office or home, reminders on a computer, or pictures showing the desired result are powerful visual reminders that condition your mind. Use whatever techniques work best for you. Remember that, at the end of the day, it boils down to *you* being accountable to *you*.

Review

Revisit your goals from time to time, evaluate where you are, make necessary adjustments, and continue toward achieving your goals. Some of your goals may seem formidable. It is not unusual to have periods of self-doubt, so don't be discouraged if you experience setbacks along the way. Stumbling blocks are bound to be encountered, especially with long-term goals. Accept up front that there will be difficulties and obstacles along the way. Develop "what if" scenarios, and anticipate ahead of time how you will deal with them, knowing that you will have to go through them or around them. Either way, you will persevere.

It is important to maintain a positive mindset. Look back at the progress you have made meeting certain objectives in pursuit of your goals. Progress is a source of self-motivation. It indicates that you are moving in the right direction and will enable you to more effectively deal with setbacks. Resolve to continue moving forward, step by step, until you get there. Once goals are achieved, they will likely be replaced by others. Just as you evolve, so will your circumstances and environment. Therefore, be aware of the dynamics, and adapt to these changes as necessary. The revision and replacement of goals should reflect this reality.

As you pursue your goals, bear in mind that few things worth anything come easily. Success does not happen overnight. It isn't handed to you. You are not entitled to success, and talent alone is no guarantee. It must be earned. If you look at the success stories in business, sports, or entertainment, you see simply the end result. You do not see the countless hours of work, frustration, failure, and adversity required.

Your hard work and perseverance will get you through it. If you are committed to something you believe in, the hard work and the struggle will be easier to endure, and the satisfaction upon reaching your goals will be far greater. However, as Henry Ford of Ford Motor Company stated, "You can't build a reputation on what you are *going* to do." The sooner you get started, the sooner you get there. The time is now. So, when setting goals, remember the five steps:

1. *Establish:* Set professional and personal goals. Stretch yourself.

2. *Define:* Be SMART.

3. *Prioritize:* List your goals by order of importance.

4. *Document:* Documentation, accountability, and self-discipline are required.

5. *Review:* Adapt, learn, revise, and move forward.

CHAPTER FOUR

Strategy

"Stop calling it a dream. It's time to call it a plan."

"Strategy," a word of Greek origin, was initially used in the context of warfare. The term is now applied to many areas, such as politics, sports, business, and even your personal life. Later in your career—especially in positions of leadership or management, or in the case of starting your own business—you will likely be exposed to business or corporate strategy. In this chapter, we will discuss both personal and business strategy.

You may never have thought of putting together a personal strategy, and yet it is central to achieving both personal and professional success. A personal strategy will help ensure that your goals and actions are aligned; it will provide focus and direction, and it will help you become more effective in all areas of your life. This strategy acts as both a guide and source of motivation, leading to a happier, healthier, more balanced life.

A personal strategy is a road map for what you want to accomplish within a specified period of time, utilizing goals, objectives, and timelines. This road map is not fixed—it is dynamic. As you evolve and grow, so will your goals. Periodic review of this road map for success is mandatory, and as you check off some goals, you will add others to reflect future ambitions.

A personal strategy should encompass a number of goals that can be divided into three main areas. The first is personal, the second is professional, and the third—which is commonly ignored—is fitness. Personal goals are related to relationships, parenting, finance, education, business, the community, and spirituality. *Personal* goals should reflect your values and what you see as your mission in life. *Professional* goals relate to what you want to accomplish in the workplace and cover a broad spectrum of possibilities. "Fitness" goals refer to your mind and body. There are many benefits to physical exercise: it alleviates stress, instills a positive attitude, gives you more energy, improves your self-image, and projects a better you to your family, friends, colleagues, and acquaintances. Personal fitness goals should never be optional.

The first step in developing a personal strategy is to do a self-assessment. List your interests, strengths, and weaknesses, and consider what you want to do. If you feel you don't yet know what your strengths and weaknesses are, let your interests guide you while you explore various opportunities—your aptitudes will present themselves. Remember that everyone has their own unique abilities and talents. It is your responsibility to leverage your strengths and become the very best you can in order to differentiate yourself in your chosen field. Involve others in this assessment, e.g., parents, spouses, friends, and trusted advisors. Get their opinion, since others can often see things you cannot.

When developing your personal strategy, give some thought to the goals, the objectives for these goals, and the tactics or actions you will employ to attain them. These goals should reflect your values and aspirations. Focus on what you can control, ensuring that the goals are realistic and attainable. Deadlines are important. If you have a goal but don't give yourself a deadline, there is a good chance you will never attain that goal. Consider what qualities and skills you have that will be helpful to your career, how transferable they are, and how you can leverage them to achieve success in your chosen field. Look at your weaknesses and what actions you can take to improve in these areas so they do not become a liability and thwart your ability to attain your goals. Consider what skills you may be missing to get to where you want to be in the future. Invest the time and effort to master these areas for the future stages of your career.

If you are entrepreneurial in nature and plan to start up your own business, you need to look at the common characteristics of successful companies. First, they have good people. Second, strategy is not given lip service. These companies place a high priority on developing a strategic plan. The benefits of having a well-conceived business strategy are numerous and affect the entire organization, small or large. The strategy should home in on what the company is good at and how it can leverage its strengths into a sustainable competitive advantage. Being able to recognize, or even implement, an effective business strategy is highly beneficial when it comes to navigating the corporate environment or leading a company successfully. Having a strategy in place accomplishes the following:

1. Clearly defines the purpose of the company and sets the direction

2. Provides guidance to the entire management team and employees

3. Establishes realistic goals and objectives

4. Creates metrics and timelines for evaluation

5. Provides focus

6. Determines accountability

7. Sets prioritization of resources

8. Provides the basis for development of financials

9. Enables the company to take advantage of opportunities and respond to threats

10. Provides for more efficiency and better decision-making

Generally speaking, strategy in the business sector is normally developed in one of three ways. The first is a bottom-up approach, in which input is solicited and sent up the chain to leadership. In larger companies, this approach can be cumbersome and can result in an aggregation of proposed strategies that may not align with the overall company strategy.

The second approach is more centralized; company leadership develops the strategy and distributes it in a standardized format with guidelines, objectives, and performance targets. This approach is more characteristic of larger companies with a corporate office, various business units, and thousands of employees. This approach will result in a more unified approach among the various business units or teams and helps to maintain the brand consistently.

The third approach is a hybrid of the previous two. In concert with the strategies stated by leadership, the respective business units review the plan and submit their own plan with recommendations. The differences between leadership and the business units are then reviewed, discussed, and reconciled. In areas of disagreement, decisions are typically made by leadership, with everyone then moving forward in lockstep with a mutually signed-off strategy. While the final plan may not represent the entirety of what was submitted by each party, it enhances the commitment of the individuals who are charged with implementing the strategy. These iterations provide the opportunity for leadership, be it senior management or a corporate office, to receive proposals on creative and innovative strategies that otherwise may not have been considered.

Communication and feedback, in both directions, are mandatory. In order for this communication to take place, there must be an atmosphere that is conducive to every voice being heard. Meetings should be conducted with rules or guidelines in place to facilitate openness. One or two individuals should not control the floor; otherwise, participants ultimately check out of the process and will not contribute. All opinions should be respected, all interruptions avoided, and criticism should be constructive in nature. To ensure openness, the leader of each strategy-planning session must control the meeting so everyone has a chance to express an opinion.

This process applies especially when it comes to starting your own business, with a few exceptions. The formulation of the strategy is almost always accomplished with a small group, involving the founders and/or key investors. The plan must be realistic and not overly optimistic. With limited resources, including money, close attention needs to be paid to goals and objectives. Metrics and timelines must be in place and routinely reviewed, with contingency plans in place in the event of short-falls, which are often finance related. If working with a bank or investors, it is important to keep them aware of progress, with clear and crisp explanations for plans and progress moving forward. Periodically bring financial partners in for a review and update on strategy and tactics. Investors, including banks, understand there will be problems along the way. Being proactive and keeping the lines of communication open will go a long way toward fostering trust and confidence. It will enhance the ability to implement contingency plans, which, in most cases, will involve some level of financial support.

An integral part of the strategic-planning process is a SWOT analysis, which assesses the relative **S**trengths, **W**eaknesses, **O**pportunities, and **T**hreats the company faces. The most immediate and important considerations are the state of the industry in which the company is competing and the company's viability in the market relative to the competition. Each phase of the market—whether it's growing, maturing, saturated, or declining—will require different strategies as well. Market intelligence on both the environment and the competition is required on a real-time basis to adapt, as changing circumstances call for different tactics. There are also numerous factors to consider—among them economic, regulatory, societal, demographic, and political. For example, if a company is in an industry in which a large percentage of business is based on pricing set by a government agency, the company needs to stay abreast of governmental pricing and policy decisions.

The essence of any company strategy is how the company's offerings compare to the competition's, how to gain an edge, and how to sustain this edge or difference. There are three basic types of strategy.

Basic Types of Strategy

1. *Cost:* This strategy, which could also be called a cost/ leadership strategy, is implemented when the company competes based on the price of their offerings. A company must be careful to ensure that, as pricing pressures come to bear, cost-reduction initiatives do not result in a decline in performance.

2. *Differentiation:* This strategy is implemented when a company offers something which is unique, oftentimes proprietary or patented, to distinguish it from the competition. The offering could also be value based, such as offering a distinct set of services. When the customer sees this offering as something that offers value, it becomes a competitive advantage and can result in a company

being able to command a premium price. When pursuing a strategy of differentiation, a company must be in close contact with the customer to ensure what is offered continues to be unique and is of value to the customer.

3. *Niche:* With this strategy, a company will develop a distinct product or approach for a defined segment or group of customers versus going after the entire market. When deciding on this strategy, the size of the segment, the growth rate, and the number of competitors are key considerations. A company must also be wary of new market entrants, especially from companies in related markets that are mature or declining, as these larger entities will seek business elsewhere and may have the ability to invest large sums quickly to bolster their market control.

The Japanese proverb "Vision without action is a daydream; action without vision is a nightmare" nicely captures this topic. It is one thing to have a good idea or vision; it is another matter to turn that vision into reality by taking the necessary steps. Strategy and implementation are inextricably linked. Thus, it is just as important to put together a plan on how the strategy will be implemented, as a poorly implemented strategy will compromise the results.

The biggest mistakes a company makes when implementing a strategy are summarized below. These mistakes are listed in no particular order, as any one of them can be crippling to a business, with a combination of them proving fatal.

Strategy-Implementation Mistakes

1. *Lack of a Coherent Strategy:* A company promoting its advantages is not a strategy—it is a marketing function, which is only part of the overall strategy. Wanting to reach $100 million in revenue is not a strategy—it is a goal. In order to have a winning strategy, the company has to decide what it is good at and what advantages it has over the competition. There must be a distinct competence setting it apart, with an accompanying value proposition that translates to value for the customer. The company must ultimately decide on the strategy, define the plan, communicate it throughout the organization, and ensure the organization is aligned, with all activities integrated, in order to create a competitive advantage.

2. *Ignoring the Human Factor:* It is essential that, during the development of the strategy, leadership involves those who will be responsible for implementing it. People will more ardently support a plan they helped develop versus a plan that is dictated to them. Greater involvement will also give the team a better understanding of the basic underpinnings of the plan, helping them make better decisions. Leadership should trust the team to carry out the plan and give them as much autonomy to do so as possible, while also holding them accountable. Thomas Jefferson once said, "The only way to make a man trustworthy is to trust him." A company can have the best strategy in the business, but without the right people, properly trained and incentivized, it will never realize its

full potential. In today's environment, with differences between companies and competitors often blurred, the human side of the equation is more important than ever. You hired good people—now trust them.

3. *Improper Communication:* Once a strategic plan has been adopted and is ready to be implemented, a critical next step is to communicate the plan to all concerned. The plan should be conveyed in a clear and concise manner, and employees should understand the larger goals of the company, as well as the specific goals applicable to them individually. The respective leadership is responsible for leading any training or planning sessions required for bridging the gap between plan and action.

4. *Lack of Accountability:* There are specific activities that go along with implementing the strategy. Every activity associated with the strategy must have someone accountable for completion of the task. Those responsible should be empowered in order to imbue ownership and accountability, and a system should be in place to monitor goal status and completion. If no one owns it, no one is accountable.

5. *Lack of Metrics:* A plan must have a set of milestones or deadlines, also called "deliverables." This schedule or list of milestones becomes the basis for setting priorities, establishing budgets, allocating time, and making decisions. These milestones need to be specific, with clear accountability. It is the accomplishment of these

milestones that determines the success of a project and a business. Ensure that you involve the appropriate personnel in developing the schedule. Unreasonable schedules developed in a vacuum lower morale and are a significant factor in companies failing to meet key milestones.

6. *Lack of Review:* A process must be in place to determine progress, which is accomplished through a series of reviews. The frequency of these reviews is predicated upon the scope and time frame of the plan. If it is an annual plan, monthly reviews—with more in-depth quarterly reviews—are recommended. This frequent monitoring will enable the company to assess progress and make the necessary adjustments. From a psychological standpoint, completion of small steps toward the greater goal is motivating to those involved, as progress—and their role in it—is acknowledged by leadership.

7. *Incentives Not Aligned:* Incentives should drive individual performance to execute a plan successfully. The plan should include incentives for both short- and long-term goals, all of which are aligned so that individual or group rewards cannot be realized at the expense of company results. While money is important, there are also intrinsic factors that motivate people. A blend of incentives addressing both components is desirable. The plan should be clearly communicated and easily understood, with full transparency.

8. *Poor Intelligence or Data:* Some of the biggest blunders in history were due to poor intelligence. The same holds true in the business arena, where decisions are made based on available information. It is incumbent upon the company leadership to ensure they have as much valid data as possible when making a decision. How they get the data is a function of company size and resources. A smaller company may not be able to invest significantly in this area, instead using its sales force and customers as sources of input, as well as outside entities specializing in market research.

When assessing data or input, one must strive to validate the data as much as possible before making decisions. Different people may characterize situations in different ways due to an inherent or organizational bias. Customers may not always express what they think, due to the way the question is phrased or simply because they do not want to offend anyone. When seeking input from customers, ensure that you create an environment that is conducive to constructive criticism and not groupthink.

As it pertains to market data or trends, it is not uncommon for companies to tout, even exaggerate, certain accomplishments when talking to commercial or industry media. When reading these reports, drawing conclusions, or trying to extrapolate data, ensure that the information is valid, and avoid coming to erroneous conclusions based on incorrect data. By the same token, be cognizant of trends or shifts you perceive in advance of data that may trail actual results. If you sense something, trust your instincts, and follow up to ensure that any subsequent actions have the proper basis to them.

9. *Strategy Conflicts With Finance:* I was in a divisional review once with other divisional managers, the president, and the senior vice president of Corporate Finance. Being a new division manager, I was very much in a listen-and-learn mode. After several presentations, I posed this question: "What is more important to you this year—profit or market share?" There was an awkward pause before the Senior Vice President of Finance fielded the question. He responded, "That is a good question. Of course, you need to make a profit; otherwise, the business is not viable, but you do not want to lose market share." I then asked, "Between the two, which one do you prefer?" The SVP paused for a moment and responded, "Both, with neither one at the expense of the other."

With that question clarified, the meeting went on. Further compounding this issue, the division managers were in a matrix-type organization, with their incentive plan based largely on the number of units sold, while the field sales organization, which had a different reporting structure, was incentivized solely on margin or profit. Consequently, on more than one occasion, there were conflicting views on what was best for the business, since the incentives were not aligned. It made for some interesting times and challenging conversations, as each side had their own perspective. It required some give and take, but, as with all things, with an open dialogue and a desire to reach common ground, compromises were reached. This was a good learning experience, as it reinforced the need to look at situations from different perspectives and aided in the development of negotiation skills. Eventually the company modified the incentive plans, thereby reducing the conflict, resulting in a more efficient process. This demonstrated the value of having an incentive plan with interests aligned.

10. *Lack of Simplicity:* The antithesis of "simplicity" is "complexity." As a company grows, takes on more offerings, adds personnel, creates new positions, and implements systems to manage growth, an unintended consequence is that business processes become more complicated. The inevitable introduction of new technologies, which require training and process adjustments, adds another layer of complexity. All of this diminishes the focus on the mission, misdirecting energy and time. An ever-growing number of individuals is involved in the process of information dissemination, which exacerbates decision-making, resulting in lengthy decision times as well as indecisiveness. Everyone is busier, but more time and effort are spent on processes that do not contribute to the overall mission, with productivity suffering. It gets "complicated." "If you can't explain it simply, you don't know it well enough," Albert Einstein is claimed to have said. When you hear a person say, "It's complicated,"

it usually means he or she either does not understand a topic well enough to explain it or is not capable of succinctly articulating it—neither one of which is a desirable trait.

If you are presented with a complex array of circumstances and do not grasp the basic issues at first pass, this is a warning sign—tread carefully, and trust your instincts. In business, even in one's personal life, the need for simplicity should be front and center. With every degree of separation, there is a degree of uncertainty; without simplicity and clarity, the chance for human error and variation increases. Review all processes, offerings, approvals, and communications with the intent to simplify and streamline as much as is practical. This is a continual process, and everyone should be involved, especially those individuals carrying out the necessary actions.

The decision process is one of the most time-consuming and frustrating aspects to many in the business world. Streamline and delegate the process as much as possible. You hire good people, so you should trust them and give them the responsibility, authority, and accountability to do their jobs. If they make good decisions, it is because they understand the plan and the parameters, and have been well trained. If they do not make good decisions, then it is because one of these ingredients is missing. The fault may, in some instances, lie not with the individual, but with the company. Determine which of the parameters are missing, and adjust accordingly.

"The supreme excellence is simplicity," the great American poet Henry Wadsworth Longfellow stated. As you go through the personal- or business-strategy process, keep the following in mind:

1. *Comprehensiveness:* Develop a strategy that includes your personal, professional, and fitness goals.

2. *Discipline:* Be determined, resolute, and proactive.

3. *Company:* Focus on differentiation and sustainability.

4. *Success Criteria:* Heed the ten essential characteristics for success.

5. *Strategy Pitfalls:* Avoid the ten common mistakes, and keep it simple.

CHAPTER FIVE

Commit

"We cannot become what we want by remaining who we are."

"Commitment to Excellence" is a motto Al Davis used to characterize the mindset of his Oakland Raiders football team. This is the mindset that must reside in each individual in order to continually elevate their game and reach desired goals.

Goals are achieved by committing to—not just being interested in—doing something. Goals require unyielding resolve, self-control, and passionate belief in your vision. You must be one hundred percent committed to moving forward, no matter what obstacles you encounter, or you will inevitably sabotage yourself. And you cannot merely *hope* things will work out. Hope is not a strategy; it is a byproduct of commitment. When you pin your prospects on *hoping* something will work out, you are planting a seed of doubt and conditioning your mind to accept something other than the desired outcome. Being fully committed results in a stronger sense of purpose and improved ability to focus. It strengthens your mindset until the thought of not attaining your goals is simply too much to bear. You will continue to push forward.

Once you commit, you are accountable to yourself. Consider this a promise to yourself, one that cannot be broken. Remember that what you do affects those around you, so share your plan with others, imparting an even greater sense of accountability. These individuals should be supportive and trustworthy, so avoid the doom-and-gloomers.

Be clear on what you want to do and what is needed to achieve your goals. If you do not have the necessary skills or tools, do you at least understand what you need to do to acquire them? Are you confident in your ability to complete the necessary steps? Do you have the resources, and if not, how do you get them? Anticipate the obstacles you may encounter and how you will deal with them. Recognize the effort and sacrifices you will have to make. This makes you better prepared and less likely to be derailed. Of course, you cannot anticipate everything— there will be some surprises, so condition yourself to find a way around them.

People and organizations relate best to those who are good at what they do. While this statement is simple, it is multifaceted, and "getting good" is no small feat. It will involve training and conditioning, and will require discipline, hard work, and time.

How much time and effort will this take? A cheeky answer might be, "Until you get good at it." A more specific answer could be "Ten thousand hours." Where did that number come from? Psychologist K. Anders Ericsson, at Berlin's Academy of

Music, conducted a study in which he classified various groups of performers by their skill level to determine what separated the top performers from the merely average. The results of the study were striking insofar as he found one common denominator, and that was how hard the individual works. In other words, the top performers put in more time. Later, based on other studies, ten thousand hours of practice was identified as being the benchmark. While this study largely concerned performers in music and sports, it reinforces the point that, if you want to get good at something, you must invest the time and effort to get there. Osmosis doesn't apply, and simply winging it doesn't work, either.

The same premise applies in sports when someone is referred to as a "natural" athlete. Using "natural" as an adjective implies that an individual is already good without practice. Although studies have shown factors such as genetics and environment can affect athletic potential, a predisposition or being a "natural" is not what enables you to get to the highest levels of performance. The common factor is not potential—it is the culmination of extra time, extra effort, and conditioning, both physically and mentally. So, if you think you are a "natural" and can take a shortcut around the hard work, don't expect success to happen any time soon.

In the military and in sports, every task and objective has a routine or process associated with it. These processes are established to reinforce and further the plan to reach a goal. Training and conditioning instill the mindset needed to optimize prospects for success because they are interconnected. "Train your body, and the mind will follow," or "Train the mind, and the body will follow," are two popular sayings. Which one is correct? Arguably, both are—but the mindset, above all, instills the will needed and acts as the shoulders of Atlas doing the heavy lifting. "Fatigue makes cowards of us all." This statement acknowledges the importance of physical training in conditioning the body and mind, and the detrimental impact poor training can have on your performance. It doesn't mean you become a coward. It simply means that, when you get to this state, you may lose your resolve, may not be as sharp or creative, and may suffer self-doubt. Consequently, your mindset will be affected. You'll start making mistakes. You will become hesitant, unsure, and fearful of taking the next step.

Studies have shown that there is a direct correlation between fitness and being productive in the workplace. When physically fit, you have more energy, concentration, creativity, sharper memory, and self-confidence. Fitness is a stress reliever and promotes good health, stimulating that all-important positive attitude.

The need for training and conditioning also holds true for your work habits and lifestyle. Burning the candle at both ends is a self-defeating practice and will ultimately catch up with you. While one can handle short bursts of overwork, a long-term regimen like this is not a formula for success. A healthy balance is important. At the Naval Academy, part of selection and training involves what is called the "whole person concept," with emphasis on the importance of being well-rounded and well-trained mentally, physically, and spiritually. An individual who keeps all three of these areas in balance is more productive, more efficient, and a better teammate.

As you move forward with your training and conditioning, adopt routines and processes that reinforce your progress toward attaining your goals. Every day, the small steps you take move you closer to achieving your goals.

As a means of reinforcement, adopt a ritual or a mantra as a continual reminder of your commitment, such as "I've got this," or "I will get this done." Place pictures or notes in common areas that are constant reminders of your commitment.

Everyone has their own definition of success, and many of us have lofty goals. While it is important to dream big, assess your objectives occasionally to ensure that they are realistic. Otherwise, you may be setting yourself up for failure and disappointment. As the plan is developed and executed, take the required steps in a consequent and deliberate manner. Brick by brick, you will build and fortify your foundation.

The commitment you are making takes time and effort. Be cognizant of those activities and demands that divert you from your plan. Keep distractions to a minimum—you will have to learn to say "No" to others, as there is nothing more valuable than your time.

When you encounter an obstacle, instead of saying, "I don't know what to do," say, "I will figure this out." Be open-minded about how to deal with setbacks, and use all resources at your disposal. Often, it is not having the answer but knowing where to find it that will provide the solution. Do not spend time trying to solve problems you cannot control; focus on what is in your control. These lessons you learn will strengthen your resolve and bolster your confidence.

Legendary football coach Vince Lombardi once said, "The quality of a person's life is in direct proportion to their commitment to excellence, regardless of their chosen field of endeavor." As you commit yourself to excellence, keep the following in mind:

1. *One hundred percent:* Commit fully—no half measures.

2. *Clarity:* Be clear, and define what you will do.

3. *Regimen:* Adopt a routine; establish good habits; be disciplined.

4. *Time:* Put the time in for training and conditioning.

5. *Three Rs:* Be realistic, resourceful, and resilient.

PART TWO

Associate With Successful People and Organizations

*"If you hang out with chickens, you're going to cluck;
if you hang out with eagles, you're going to fly."*

—Steve Mariboli

CHAPTER ONE

Act

"The difference between who you are and who
you want to be is what you do."

"Action is the foundational key to all success," is a quotation
attributed to Pablo Picasso. Any plan, desire, or goal must be
acted upon for it to come to fruition. However, as we have seen
and likely experienced, the action necessary to achieve a goal or
realize an ambition oftentimes never happens in the first place.
How many times have you had a conversation with someone who
expresses regret over an action not taken or a path not pursued?

"What if?" There have been times when you have posed this
question to yourself or have heard others express the same senti-
ment with respect to a path not taken. There are myriad reasons
for stalling, holding back, and not taking action. They usually
include at least one of five reasons: resistance to change, fear, lack
of confidence, lack of discipline, or lack of time. Acknowledging

that these issues exist and creating strategies to address these barriers are central to fulfilling your potential.

Humans are creatures of habit. We have our routine, we get used to doings things a certain way, and we usually have a circle of friends who reinforce our own beliefs and values. It is very difficult for some of us to alter that routine and to step out of that comfort zone. Our circle of friends, many of whom are like-minded, will find fault with anything that disrupts the status quo. Therefore, potential negative consequences outweigh the benefits of any change; the status quo is justified, and we do not venture outside our comfort zone. The longer we stay in our comfort zone, the more emotionally attached we become to it, making it that much harder to take that next step.

Reluctance to change is not abnormal. Some people are better equipped to handle change due to upbringing and previous experience. Conversely, others are not readily predisposed to change due to their past experience, resulting in a bias toward inaction. Whether you are equipped to handle change or not, change is a constant in your life. You must accept that change is inevitable. You have to force yourself out of your comfort zone and embrace change as an opportunity instead of a threat. Rather than focusing on the negative consequences, focus on the positive aspects, understanding that change presents a chance for personal and professional growth. You can condition yourself by first starting with the small changes, gaining confidence along the way. Later you will look back and be glad you took that first step, understanding that *"movement is life."*

Fear comes in various shapes and sizes and can encompass a host of issues or scenarios. It is a perfectly normal response to a perceived threat. Fear triggers our "fight or flight" response, which has been honed by thousands of years of evolution. While the threats have changed over the years and are now more psychological than physical, they are present nonetheless. Fear has probably killed more dreams than failure and is perhaps the single biggest reason for someone not reaching their potential.

Avoidance is not a winning strategy for dealing with fear—it will only make things worse. You must face your fear head on; running away is not an option, despite discomfort and unpleasant emotions. One strategy for coping with this fear is to repeatedly put yourself in these situations. As a result, you will condition your mind and your body to overcome these fears through a process known as desensitization.

For example, if you are fearful of public speaking, the best strategy is to develop your skills for presenting through practice and visualization, and then put yourself out there. Take every opportunity you can to give a speech or a presentation. Over time, your fear will dissipate, and you'll find that it really is not that bad after all. You'll gain experience that will buttress your confidence, thus turning a liability into an asset.

Of the five reasons often listed for not taking action, confidence in oneself is inextricably linked to the first two and is a primary contributor to inaction and failure. If you are not confident, or if you don't believe in yourself, how can you get anything done, and how can you expect anyone else to believe in you? Successful people all have one trait in common: they believe in themselves and are confident in their ability to succeed.

A lack of confidence allows fear to hold you back from pursuing your dreams and achieving your goals. This fear will also influence you to make poor choices, as your decisions will be based on outcomes you want to avoid, rather than those you desire. This cycle of inaction and misdirection breeds more fear, more inaction, becoming a self-fulfilling prophecy.

Confidence is not an inherited trait. It is developed and acquired over time. And yes, you absolutely can do something about it if you take control and commit to taking the necessary measures. Here is what you need to do and how to do it.

Building Your Confidence

1. *Assess:* Look inside yourself. What do you see as your limitations or shortcomings? Where do you need to improve in order to take action and pursue your goals? What is holding you back? Don't hesitate to seek feedback from those whose opinions you trust and value.

2. *Plan:* Once you have decided what areas you need to work on, put together a plan. The plan should list actions you will take to work on specific areas. If you need to venture outside your comfort zone, be prepared to do it, since it is only by stretching yourself that you can grow.

3. *Start small:* There is no quick fix. A series of small successes over time will give you the experience and courage needed to move on to bigger challenges. You need to have the resolve to stick to the plan and the resiliency to handle minor setbacks.

4. *Increase competence:* "*Ex Scientia Tridens*" is the motto of the Naval Academy and translates to "from knowledge, sea

power." A good motto for this part would be *"Ex Scientia Fiduciam,"* or "from knowledge, confidence." It is incumbent upon you to become knowledgeable and well versed in all aspects of your chosen profession. Your proficiency will make you better prepared and more confident.

5. *Prepare:* Planning and preparation are the keys to success. If you have not studied, you will not be very confident going into the test. The same holds true for everything you undertake. The more prepared you are, the more confidence you have in your ability.

6. *Focus on the positive:* Maintain a positive mental attitude. Where the mind goes, the body follows. The more positive you think, the more positive the results. Visualization can be a powerful motivational tool. Take the time to mentally rehearse projecting positive thoughts and a positive outcome. Other people will also more strongly relate to you when you project a strong, positive self-image.

7. *Don't dwell on the negative:* Focus on the things that go right and possibilities of success, rather than past failures or the possibility of failure. Purge negative thoughts from your brain so you do not psyche yourself out. Evaluate those people you associate with who are largely negative. They do nothing for anyone's confidence or self-esteem and only bring you down.

8. *Maintain a consistent image:* Most communication is nonverbal, with many people forming an opinion about

someone within thirty seconds of meeting them. These first impressions are long-lasting, with a positive first impression going a long way to ensuring a positive relationship or outcome. Be attentive to your body language. Stand tall, hold your head high, make eye contact, and smile while offering a firm handshake. Depending upon your business or environment, grooming standards and dress are obvious considerations.

9. *Exercise:* I am a big proponent of exercise and subscribe to the tenet that "Exercise is medicine." Exercise affects several areas in a positive way, e.g., less stress, increased focus, and higher energy. Overall, exercise helps project a more positive self-image.

10. *Review and revise:* Improvement in any regard is a continuum. You must never stand still. You must have the willpower to take action, to commit to continually reviewing progress, and to make adjustments as you grow personally and professionally.

George Washington stated, "Discipline is the soul of an army. It makes small numbers formidable, procures success to the weak, and esteem to all." By the same token, discipline is the soul of your journey; it is one of the most important traits required for success in whatever you strive to accomplish. This discipline will enable you to remain steadfast and resolute, giving you the freedom to go where you want to go and be what you want to be.

Discipline gives you the will to take the necessary actions to improve yourself, the courage to get outside of your comfort zone and face your fears, and the self-control to stick to a regimen. A lack of discipline results in procrastination and excuses and distracts you from doing what is necessary to achieve success. You'll fail to face the challenges that need to be confronted, resulting in missed opportunities. You will become stagnant, never stepping outside of your comfort zone, and relegating yourself to a lifetime of mediocrity.

As with any other process, discipline is a learned behavior, and actions can be taken to improve your self-discipline. To learn this behavior, take the following steps.

Developing Self-Discipline

1. Define what you want to do and why you want to do it. Develop a plan with specific goals and timelines. Start with smaller goals that are achievable, which will help you build confidence as you commence your new routine.

2. Identify the obstacles or stressors you will encounter and how you will deal with them. Anticipate, visualize, and overcome. Put yourself in your discomfort zone, as this will condition you to act more effectively in these situations.

3. Develop a routine, and stick with it. This is not unlike a routine that athletes will follow. Train and condition yourself to become more disciplined, and it will become second nature.

4. Track your progress by routinely reviewing your plan. This helps you stay focused. Accept that setbacks will occur along the way.

5. Make the commitment to follow through with your plan. Hold yourself accountable. Get rid of your excuses.

Adhering to this regimen will result in your new approach becoming ingrained. Over time, as small successes mount up, bad habits are abandoned, good habits are developed, and you take control.

Accomplishing goals to realize your vision is a time-consuming process. It does not happen overnight. In a culture of instant gratification, it can be very difficult for someone to dedicate the time that will be required. How often have you heard someone say, "I don't have enough time"? That is often code for "I am not organized, and I don't know how to plan."

Throughout this learning process, you must be willing to dedicate the time and effort required to realize your goals. You will need to plan, manage your time, avoid distractions, and not fall back on a bevy of excuses as an avoidance tactic. Having a strong belief in what you are doing will give you the will and strength of conviction to follow through. Get into an action mode, and remember the following:

1. *Confront:* Face your fears; allow no excuses; get out of your comfort zone.

2. *Confidence:* Develop yourself; improve your self-image; increase your proficiency.

3. *Discipline:* It starts with you. Follow the plan, and stick with it.

4. *Be Positive:* Maintain a positive mindset; where the mind goes, the body follows.

5. *Manage:* Manage the plan and your time. Stay focused, and avoid distractions.

CHAPTER TWO

Learn

"It never gets easier. You just get better."

"Tell me and I forget. Teach me and I remember. Involve me and I learn," stated Benjamin Franklin regarding the learning process. Regardless of what you do in life, or what career you pursue, learning is a continual quest. Even after concluding formal education or technical training, you should strive to increase your knowledge and proficiency. Each year, two-thirds of all U.S. workers, in order to remain competent and competitive in their field, take a course or receive further training to stay abreast of current developments and enhance their skills. Many take further training to gain an edge and improve their prospects for career advancement. Learning is a continuum, an ongoing process. Many do not fully appreciate that learning is also a skill, and, with greater attention to the learning process, you will learn and retain more, increasing your competence and confidence.

Methods

Learning is accomplished through either passive or active means. Reading, attending lectures, listening to recordings, and watching a video are examples of passive learning. Discussions, demonstrations, real-life experience, and on-the-job training are examples of active learning. All of these techniques have their place, with varying retention rates. Some people learn better in an auditory manner, others in a visual manner, and others through hands-on experience.

Passive-learning methods have a lower retention rate. This is partly a byproduct of how the brain best learns, which is different for everyone. However, regardless of what works best for you, there are techniques to improve your learning and retention. If you are in a classroom setting, rather than typing your notes on a computer, be a little old-fashioned, and write the notes longhand. Studies have shown that, while typing on a keyboard, your ability to grasp the higher concepts of the information is compromised, as so much of your time and attention is devoted to the mechanical process of typing. Once your notes are completed in handwritten form, review them, and type them up, preferably in outline form. This process presents the information to you again, offering further reinforcement. If some of the learning is based on audio recordings or videos, listen or watch them repeatedly, even taking notes as you go along.

Instead of cramming at the last minute, make the time to periodically review your notes to further embed this information.

Learning spread out over time, combined with repetition, is central to converting this information from your short-term to your long-term memory. When reading a textbook or a manual, the same principles apply. Highlight key sections, even jotting down notes next to key passages. Afterward, review the highlighted sections and notes periodically, just as you do with classroom notes, as a means of reinforcement.

Active-learning methods have a higher retention rate, since you are connecting what you have already learned with real-life experience. Engaging in a group discussion or study group is an effective way to learn and retain information. Presenting information in either a classroom or informal setting is another approach, with the process of organizing the information serving to further ingrain it.

You will learn through a combination of these methods. Determine which methods work best for you, and tailor your efforts accordingly. The more on-the-job or hands-on training you get, the better, as it is one thing to take a leadership class and another thing to actually lead.

Proficiency

You may have a great plan and believe in what you are doing. However, if you are not good at what you do, you will never get anywhere. If you want to set yourself apart from your competition, being good is not enough. You need to be better and become as proficient as possible in your chosen field to be seen as an expert and an individual who gets results. You need to work not only on your job but also on yourself. Focus on your strengths, be strategic about what skills you need to develop, and then develop them.

Everyone is dealing with the same issues, but many do not have the focus, self-discipline, and determination to follow through and do what is necessary to lift themselves above the fray. The first thing to do is dive deeply into what you are doing and learn as much as possible about it, in as many ways as possible, from a variety of viewpoints.

Read as much as you can, talk to as many people as you can, and seek the advice of experts. As you begin exploring your chosen career, learn as much as possible about the products or services your industry offers, familiarizing yourself with their purpose, and get customer perspectives to understand what is important to them. Learn as much as you can about your competition, and stay abreast of industry trends. If or whenever possible, attend conferences and seminars, take additional classes, and establish a network of trusted advisors.

Challenge yourself. Do not hesitate to put yourself in challenging situations and take on demanding projects. Stretch your limits, create pressure, and even fear. While this is not easy, you will grow and expand as you expose yourself to new situations and new ways of thinking. Put yourself in a position where you are forced to succeed. This process, while uncomfortable, will change you for the better, as getting out of your comfort zone is an essential ingredient to growth.

Mentor

The recipe for success is a combination of ingredients encompassing education, training, proficiency, communication, interpersonal skills, hard work, and resilience. One ingredient in this recipe that is often overlooked is the importance of a mentor, a common denominator for most people who have been successful.

There are various definitions of a "mentor." In the traditional sense, a mentor is someone who is older and more experienced than you are, has achieved success, offers guidance, and provides insight. Often, this person is within your chosen industry or field, but that does not always have to be the case.

Mentors are invaluable since they have "been there, done that" and have real-life learning experience that cannot be gleaned from a textbook. They have experienced successes, adversity, and failures, and have encountered circumstances that may be similar to what you will face. With their counsel, you can learn from their experience, gain a better understanding of what issues you will encounter, avoid making the same mistakes, and employ proven tactics to resolve issues you encounter.

Mentors do not fall out of the sky; they happen in one of two ways. The first possibility is through a formal mentoring program, which is usually a short-term arrangement that is structured, with defined objectives. These are normally for a new employee, manager, squad member, etc., and are short-term arrangements that could turn into longer-term ones, based on the setting and circumstances. Long-term mentor arrangements, particularly in a corporate setting, need to be handled in an even-handed fashion. Politics or personalities could come into play, with questions of objectivity or favoritism possibly arising. Even if this isn't the case, perception is reality.

In the absence of a formal program, a mentoring relationship may not develop at a precise time or point in your career;

they will evolve as relationships are made, friendships are forged, and you get to know more people. It may be someone who sees something in you and takes you under their wing, or it could be the result of you asking someone for advice—a common means of mentor establishment. This is done by taking the initiative and asking for advice. Later, you will ask again, and, over time, if there is mutual respect and chemistry, a bond will be formed.

The mentor's views will sometimes be different from yours, as they provide unique insight based on their experience. This second set of eyes and ears gives you a valuable perspective, enabling you to better connect the dots and bridge the gap between perception and reality, which could be the difference between success and failure.

You may also end up with a number of informal arrangements and a handful of mentors or advisors. Depending on the subject, you can ask more than one for advice. It usually goes something to the effect of, "What would you recommend?" "Do you think I should do this?" "What do I need to look out for?" or "Can I bounce something off you?" If there is a consensus as you sift through their remarks, this is a good sign; it reinforces the fact you are headed in the right direction. If there isn't a consensus, and more questions are raised than answered, it is a warning sign: tread carefully.

A good mentor should be someone who not only offers advice and encouragement but also provides unfiltered feedback and constructive criticism. Constructive criticism comes with the territory and should be taken in the same manner it was given, even though it sometimes can be difficult to hear. Years ago, prior to a football game in high school, my coach was riding me incessantly. This went on all week, and it seemed I could do nothing right; my footwork was faulty, I was taking too long to release the ball, I wasn't picking up the secondary receiver quickly enough, and so forth. Finally, the day before the game, I decided to confront my coach. I went up to him and said, "Dad, what am I doing wrong? You have been on me all week." He looked at me and said, "Son, you shouldn't worry about me yelling. You should worry when I stop, because that means I don't care." I have always remembered that conversation, and if you ever find yourself in a similar situation with a trusted advisor, bear in mind that they are trying to make you better.

Technology

Not so long ago, a student would walk into a classroom with a notebook and a pencil. Today that student walks in with a smartphone and a laptop. Technology has had a profound impact on the education landscape, changing how we are taught and learn. In addition to learning the subject matter, one must also learn about the technology and understand how to use it in an effective and efficient manner. For those exposed to digital technology at a young age, the technology learning curve is not steep. For those who weren't, the learning curve can be a challenge and an impediment when considering jobs or careers. If you ever find yourself uncomfortable with a new technology that pertains to your chosen field, you need to get comfortable with it, so that it does not thwart career opportunities. Technology training is a booming industry, and there are courses offered by any number of organizations. Determine what you need to learn or improve upon, do some research, ask around, and find the courses that will get you up to speed.

Whether in school, out of school, or working, there are several ways for you to augment and continue the learning process. Distance learning, even online degree programs, are increasingly prominent and commonplace with most colleges and universities. If you have geographic limitations or time constraints, distance-learning options offer the opportunity to pursue learning that otherwise would not be available. They also permit you to learn at your own pace while augmenting your knowledge to further your proficiency. Other methods include web-based seminars, podcasts, and online tutorials. Mobile learning opportunities have expanded more than anything else via the use of smartphones, laptops, and iPads, which provide access to several learning options available at your convenience. With the abundance of opportunities for education and further learning, there is no excuse for not getting the education or training you need, as barriers which existed before have been broken. Once again, the ball is in your court, so take the initiative.

Throughout this entire process, keep in mind that technology is a means to an end, not an end in itself. It is a tool to facilitate your learning, not to replace learning. The creativity and innovation come from you, not from the technology. It is up to you to learn how to leverage the technology in the most practical and effective manner. Remember, even with all this remote learning and technology, it ultimately comes down to people talking to people for decisions to get made.

Plan

You have an arsenal of methods for learning at your disposal, you want to increase your proficiency, and you have already established personal and professional goals. The next step is to look at where you want to be in both the short-term and in the long-term, and how you match up with those currently in the position or profession you aspire to. Research what skills, competencies, or certifications are required. How do you get them, and when do you get them? Put together a list along with specific actions, a timeline, and milestones. Identify any barriers that exist. How will you overcome them? Look at your weaknesses as well, and come up with strategies to turn them into strengths. Discuss your plan with your mentor, if you have one, to get ideas and support.

Regardless of what support network you have, it is ultimately up to you to make this plan come to fruition. Take the following steps:

1. *Method:* Learn how you learn best; spread out learning; employ repetition.

2. *Proficiency:* Become an expert; dig deep; challenge yourself.

3. *Mentor:* Find one or more, and listen to them.

4. *Technology:* Understand it and how to use it.

5. *Plan:* Identify and attain the skills and competencies you will need.

Quotients

"Your success in life will largely be determined
by your EQ, rather than your IQ."

"Individual effort to a group effort—that is what makes a team work, a company work, a society work, and a civilization work," Vince Lombardi stated. Whatever you do or wherever you work, human dynamics will always be an integral part of the equation, in any field or discipline.

You must be able to work with others, to understand them, respect them, trust them, to value their perspective, to have their back when necessary—and you must work within that system to be effective and successful.

America has long been noted for a strong spirit, a sense of individuality, and a penchant for personal responsibility, which has been a catalyst for creativity and innovation. Most of the great American inventions and discoveries entailed one or two individuals working independently and relentlessly until they achieved a breakthrough. Some of this was born out of necessity, as communication and transportation were not as accessible and rapid as they are today. There was no Internet, and travel time was measured in weeks and months, not hours or days. Companies were more regional or national in nature, the population was lower, and the workforce was homogenous.

Fast forward to today. With the Internet and modern technology, communication is rapid, with the only limiting factor being the time zone. Rapid forms of travel have broken down geographic barriers. The growing population, combined with advances in technology, have resulted in a vastly different, borderless workplace. You are just as likely to be working with someone across the country as you are with someone halfway across the world as business becomes globalized. More companies are no longer only regional or national in scope and have footprints on other continents. The workforce is highly diverse, with many projects being collaborative in nature and involving individuals with varied backgrounds and expertise.

These dynamics have resulted in a paradigm shift in analytics, as companies and organizations are looking at other factors as a predictive measure of employability and likelihood of success. This has given rise to a new science that assesses how well a person can work with other people. In former times, it was called "people skills," but today it is called "emotional quotient" and is considered a skill. "Emotional quotient" is sometimes used interchangeably with the term "emotional intelligence," but this is incorrect, as they are entirely different terms. It also differs from another popular quotient, called "IQ," or "intelligence quotient."

The IQ test is a standardized test developed in the early 1900s. The purpose of the test was to measure someone's intelligence, with the test score being used for educational placement, learning purposes, and as a predictor for general success in life. The basic reasoning was that someone who was smarter would make better decisions and have greater prospects for success in their chosen endeavor. In the absence of any other metric, the IQ was the standard test for decades. However, it is now recognized that having a high IQ is not always an accurate indicator of success. The consensus among experts is that one's IQ contributes to ten to twenty percent of their success, with other factors being better success predictors. These factors have come to the forefront due to the changing nature of business and the growing awareness that someone who cannot work effectively with others will have difficulty working as part of a team, let alone being in a leadership position.

The concept of considering one's emotional makeup was first addressed in the 1800s. "Emotional intelligence" was coined as a measurement of an individual's ability to understand and manage their emotions and behavior. The term "emotional quotient" has subsequently evolved as a means to assess not only someone's emotional intelligence but how that individual works with others. The remainder of this chapter will use the terminology "emotional quotient" or "EQ," using the descriptive term or abbreviation interchangeably.

There is no skill or trait more important than your emotional quotient. EQ refers to your capacity to work with others, to understand them and relate to them, and your ability to use this awareness to be effective in your workplace and environment.

Think of EQ as the emotional equivalent of the IQ. Many companies test and screen for EQ and place a higher value on someone's emotional quotient than their IQ. They realize that a high IQ devoid of emotional maturity is not a winning combination. Your success will be determined by approximately eighty percent EQ and twenty percent or less IQ.

Emotional quotient consists of the sum of acuity in five key areas.

Key Traits of Emotional Quotient

1. *Self-awareness:* This refers to the ability to understand your emotions, drives, strengths, and weaknesses, as it is only by understanding them that you can manage them. It is also a reflection of your ability to assess the dynamics of what is transpiring, assess the emotions of others, and understand the impact you have on them. Self-awareness is key for people to be confident in themselves and with others. Understanding that they are not perfect helps them realize and make peace with the fact that they make mistakes. They accept constructive criticism, take it professionally—not personally—and use it as input to improve, versus going into an emotional spiral. They are good listeners and can discern fact from fiction, as they are able to separate from emotions and bias, taking objective viewpoints. When a problem or crisis occurs, discussion and solutions are based on reasonable and objective discourse, unclouded by emotions or bias.

2. *Self-control:* "Whom the Gods destroy, they first make angry," declaimed the Greek playwright Euripides. Put another way, "Lose control of your emotions, and you'll lose control of your mind." Of all the traits that your emotional quotient comprises, self-control is the most important. If you cannot control yourself and your emotions, you will never have a healthy relationship, professionally or personally. Self-control refers to the capability to control your behavior, impulses, and reactions. People who have self-control are usually trustworthy, adaptive, committed to their work, and have a positive outlook. Being self-aware, they realize they have faults. When they make mistakes, they accept accountability and move on, avoiding the blame game and not trying to live by a different set of rules. Organizations gravitate toward levelheaded individuals like this who seem "in control" and who will rationally discuss a given situation. They are adaptable and open to new and different ways to find a solution.

3. *Motivation:* Individuals with a good EQ motivate themselves and those around them. They take pride in achieving success, not only for themselves but for the team, helping others along the way. They understand the alignment of goals, and that collective effort produces the optimum result. They commit to success, take the initiative, and are relentless, despite obstacles or setbacks. Their positive attitude is obvious through their

demeanor and their discourse, inspiring confidence and facilitating a successful outcome.

4. *Empathy:* "Understanding" is synonymous with "empathy." In a globalized business world, you will frequently deal with people from a different region, country, culture, or socio-economic background. The ability to understand, collaborate, and effectively work in a diverse workforce and customer set is not a *desired* skill—it is a *required* skill. Empathy is the ability to recognize and react compassionately to the feelings of others, while understanding and appreciating their background and circumstances. If you can relate to a given individual, this understanding sends positive signals and enhances your ability to work together and collaborate. It is a critical skill in negotiation, particularly in the international arena, as customs differ by nationality and culture. Leaders, in particular, must understand what makes certain people tick, and tailor their approach accordingly. People who possess this skill are good listeners, keeping their emotions or biases from interfering with their ability to grasp the nuances of a given situation. They are good at anticipating the needs of others; they cultivate support and garner respect across the human spectrum.

5. *Interpersonal Skills:* These are frequently referred to as "social skills," but "interpersonal" is a more appropriate term, since it applies specifically to personal relationships in any setting. Another synonymous term would

be "people skills." Interpersonal or people skills have a direct impact on success in almost any environment. People with high interpersonal skills are good communicators, work well with others, are able to "read" people, and manage conflict. They are able to wield influence and persuade others through effective communication techniques, giving credence to the saying, "It's not what you say—it's how you say it." They have a positive attitude and self-confidence, and they tend to be well-liked, fostering trust and loyalty among peers. They are excellent at negotiation and collaboration; they are adaptable and friendly; and they can easily establish a rapport, facilitating discussion and resolution of issues. Having traveled and done business in countless countries across the globe, one of my goals was always to establish a rapport or chemistry with whomever the other party may be.

I was once in a meeting in a country in Asia. It was a very large and complex project, involving myriad technology and significant financial outlay for the customer. Present at the meeting were several high-ranking government officials, including a number of high-ranking military personnel. As the meeting commenced, I was first lectured that the United States did not understand their country and that we did not have much in common. I paused and inquired if I could ask the group a question. They all nodded. I then asked, "How many of you in this room are married? Please raise your hand." They were a bit surprised. I raised my hand first, and soon everyone in the room had raised their hand. I then asked, "How many of you are the boss in your own home?" I kept my hand down at my side and looked around the room. No hands were raised; a few attendees even chuckled. I then stated, "It would seem we all have much more in common than we think we do." That broke the ice, and the meeting proceeded to a successful conclusion. While this may appear a bit unorthodox, it had the intended effect.

Until now, emotional quotient as a skill set or trait may have been foreign to you, however, its importance cannot be overstated. Some people are naturally predisposed, with some traits more resident within them than others. Fortunately, just like anything else, emotional quotient can be learned and developed. The process is different from what we've discussed previously, but the fundamentals remain the same. Take the following steps to develop your EQ:

Developing Your Emotional Quotient

1. *Self-Evaluation and Practice:* Knowing your strengths and weaknesses is the first step in improving your EQ. You can do this in several ways. Introspection and self-assessment are required—be honest with yourself. There are a number of EQ tests available online that provide further analysis and details. These can be helpful in providing a metric or baseline measurement. Get

the perspective of others, such as close friends, trusted advisors, and mentors. Sometimes we view ourselves one way while others view us differently, and it is not uncommon to hold a disproportionate view of our own strengths and weaknesses. You can use this information to put together an assessment and develop a plan. Just as one has certain physical, musical, or language skills that can be developed with training and practice, the same holds true for your EQ. There are strategies and techniques you can learn. If you need help developing a plan, do not be afraid to ask for help. You can simplify the process by prioritizing and focusing on one or two areas until you have made progress. You build on this by adding another area in tandem with your existing regimen. With practice, you will see continual improvement, but you must have the discipline to stick to your plan.

2. *Self-control:* We all experience different levels of stress. How you react in a stressful situation reveals a lot about you and greatly affects how others see you. Self-control is important for you to overcome your fears and for avoiding self-destructive behavior. Lack of control results in impulsive and negative behavior and overly emotional responses. You should identify those situations or issues that provoke impulsive and negative emotional behavior. Then, do some research. You'll find that there are various techniques and coping strategies you can employ, such as visualization, to train your mind to help manage these stressful situations. Find which ones work best for

you, practice them, and put them to use. The key is to anticipate and be proactive so you do not get caught off guard, feel overwhelmed, and react without thinking— a detrimental situation often fraught with misdirected anxiety and conflict. Ensure that you exercise and get adequate amounts of sleep to help your brain manage your energy more efficiently and avoid "decision fatigue."

3. *Stretch Yourself:* You will never realize your full potential unless you step out of your comfort zone into challenging and stressful situations. It is easy to stay comfortable and maintain a safe routine. However, this avoidance completely thwarts your personal and professional growth, evoking the adage "No pain, no gain," or, in our case, "No discomfort, no growth." By challenging yourself, you learn more about yourself. You may be surprised and realize you are able to do more than you thought, improving your confidence and self-esteem. You may also fail, but you must view failure as a lesson from which you gain knowledge that will help you succeed next time. Employ the lessons you learn to develop tactics and coping strategies. All of this enables you to be better prepared for the next challenge, making you better equipped to handle change and adversity. This is a continuum; your behavior won't change overnight, but with a resolute and determined mindset to improve, you will be surprised at what you can accomplish.

4. *Objectivity:* Epictetus, a stoic Greek philosopher, stated, "Appearances to the mind are of four kinds. Things

either are what they appear to be; or they neither are, nor appear to be; or they are, and do not appear to be; or they are not, and yet appear to be. Rightly to aim in all these cases is the wise man's task." In other words, what you read or hear may be true, not be true, be partially true, or have been taken out of context. It may be steeped in fact, fueled by rumor, or presaged by bias or malicious intentions. Sometimes the speed of the message can leave the facts in the wake of the transmission. While being decisive is a desirable trait, seek the truth, avoid rushing to judgment, and ensure you have all the facts, so that your decisions are made in a rational and objective manner. You have preconceived notions about various things, which is normal, but do not let your ideas get in the way of the flow and exchange of information. Put your feelings aside; always seek to understand the other side's viewpoint, and use this information as part of the decision-making process.

When confronted with a problematic situation, do not complain, look for someone to blame, or immediately jump to a negative conclusion. To do so portrays yourself as the victim, admitting that this is a situation beyond your control and that nothing can be done about it. This behavior does not inspire anyone and is not a quality in great demand. Be objective, solicit views from others, and do not let your personal judgment of someone cloud your thinking—their input may have merit. You will make better decisions and gain respect by taking this approach.

5. *Communication:* Effective communication requires trust. To establish trust, you must understand others and develop a relationship with them. It is much easier to go into a meeting and gain support when you have some degree of familiarity with those in the room. To do this requires empathy and confidence: the empathy to understand and appreciate the other person's viewpoint, and the confidence and interpersonal skills to forge relationships and get to know people. This is easier for some and more difficult for others, but having those abilities gives one the upper hand. Empathy allows you to relate to the other person, to read them in real time, and to adjust accordingly on the fly, enabling you to communicate more effectively. If you can relate to them, they will be able to relate to you, resulting in a more effective dialogue. A degree of emotional quotient is required to forge a connection with individuals. This may require you to step outside of your box—to take the time to initiate conversations, to learn someone's first name, their interests, what they do, etc. By taking an active interest and listening, both parties develop a better understanding of each other. These connections, built up over time, enhance familiarity, trust, and respect, all of which are necessary ingredients in overcoming resistance to change, enhancing collaboration, and fostering teamwork.

Business is simple; people are complex. Most problems or issues you will encounter are rooted in human dynamics, which affect performance and stress levels. Focusing on your emotional quotient will never make problems go away, but it will help mitigate the symptoms. The good news is that there are actions that can be taken to improve this aspect of your performance. Again, this is a continuum; you constantly work at it, and, with effort, you will realize improvement if you do the following:

1. *Assess:* Determine your EQ strengths and weaknesses. Be objective and open-minded.

2. *Plan:* Develop a strategy, including tactics and coping techniques.

3. *Regimen:* Adhere to your plan, maintaining self-control and discipline.

4. *Stretch:* Journey outside your comfort zone—no discomfort, no growth.

5. *EQ:* Make a determined effort to improve your emotional quotient and communication.

CHAPTER FOUR

Communication

"The worst distance between two people is misunderstanding."

"The single biggest problem in communication is the illusion that it has taken place," wrote famed playwright George Bernard Shaw.

Common curriculum over the span of one's formal education consists of numerous courses with common focuses, such as mathematics, science, history, chemistry, biology, and so forth, with courses becoming more specialized in higher education. However, throughout most courses of study, there is likely a lack of courses or instruction covering the topic of communication.

The ability to effectively communicate is one of the most critical skills required for someone to be successful in the business world—or anything else, for that matter, including relationships or marriage. The most effective leaders in the business or political world all have one trait in common—they are excellent communicators who can effectively convey their message, articulate the key points, and provide inspiration.

In ancient Greece and later in Rome, most mass communication took place through public speaking. The great leaders of that time were all extraordinary orators. They had the ability to convey their vision and articulate it in powerful ways, inspiring masses of listeners toward social and political change, and even military action. Knowing the importance of public oration, many of these individuals devoted a great deal of time to practicing the art of speech, focusing on tone, inflection, pronunciation, and physical gestures. It was considered an art form and was a prerequisite for success.

Not much has changed today. Whether in business, politics, or even local civic organizations, much of our communication is still done orally, in public or in private, to groups of various sizes. In many instances, however, we do not give adequate thought or preparation to the quality or content of our performance. Our remarks and delivery inevitably reflect our lack of preparation, and our message will not be met with the reception we hoped for.

There have likely been times you have seen two people propose basically the same thing, with one receiving support and positive acknowledgment, and the other denied. What was the difference? The difference was not the message—the difference was the messenger. The difference was that one person conveyed the message effectively, allowing it to be received and understood clearly, and the other person did not.

Good communication is not just desirable, it is necessary for an individual or business to be successful. This fact is amplified due to the current nature of the workforce and workflow. Most work involves a group of individuals who are formed into a team in order to collaborate on a project. The members of the team could be a cross section of individuals encompassing different disciplines from different parts of the country or world. If the team is to operate effectively, each member must have a clear understanding of his or her role as well as the desired overall outcome. For this to occur, the person in charge of this team must be not only an effective leader but also an effective communicator. It is one thing to have a good idea of how a product, service, or process can be improved; it is another to effectively and clearly communicate that idea.

Unfortunately, these qualities are not always resident within individuals in a leadership position. If these qualities are absent, the team will not be effective, the business will not be as successful, and individuals will not realize their full potential. In today's working environment, one must be able to effectively communicate across all available channels of communication—in person and in writing, including email. The individual who can do this has a distinct advantage.

In 1923, Henry Luce and his partner Briton Hadden launched *TIME* magazine. They were inspired to create *TIME* by the social changes that were taking place in the country. It was their contention that, with the increasing pace of modern life and its concordant time constraints, people would respond well to a news format that was briefer, formatted so the reader could easily find an article of interest and read it quickly. Their initial guidelines were "one hundred short articles each week, none of which are more than four hundred words in length." History has borne out the wisdom of this approach. To this day,

TIME remains the longest-running news source of its kind still in publication.

Fast-forward one hundred years to today. Consider the social changes that have taken place and the multitude of avenues for communication and information available. The changes from then to now are exponential. Attention spans have shortened, not lengthened. Consequently, when communicating, most people will respond best to messaging that is clear and to the point. All good communicators have the ability to simplify their message and convey it in such a manner that the audience grasps what is being said.

Types of Communication

There are three types of communication: oral, written, and nonverbal. Oral communication includes direct conversation between two individuals or among several people, such as one-on-one discussion, meetings, telephone discussions, presentations, lectures, and symposiums, the latter two being forms of active-passive communication. Oral communication, unless in the form of a lecture or a symposium, is typically informal, with a high degree of interpersonal involvement. It is typically highly transparent and fluid, allowing a ready exchange of information and feedback. Oral communication is best for establishing relationships, building trust, and motivating others; it is preferred for addressing issues that are complex or personal in nature. However, due to the less-structured nature of oral communication, information may be lacking or conveyed out of order, and misunderstandings can occur if the listener is inattentive or takes things out of context.

Written communication is any medium that utilizes the written word—letters, advertisements, contracts, press releases, emails, etc., including information posted publicly online. These forms of communication are frequent in the business world. Electronic media allow us to deliver messages and information instantaneously to any number of people, unbound by geography. This gives us the advantages of speed, reduced cost, permanent documentation, and the ability to reach a broad audience. However, some drawbacks include an inherent risk to privacy, a higher possibility of misinterpretation, a lack of recoverability—clicking "Send" cannot be taken back—and a tendency to be used inappropriately, e.g., topics that have no business being discussed digitally.

More than fifty percent of all human communication is done nonverbally, or physically, making it the predominant way we exchange information. Nonverbal communication is crucial to the communication process, yet many fail to understand this importance or are simply unaware of their own nonverbal behavior. This includes body language, facial expressions, eye contact, mannerisms, and attire. Others continuously assess and make determinations based on these factors, and thus, much of your success will depend how you communicate nonverbally.

Effective communication is a valuable skill in the workplace, as a large portion of our day is spent interacting and communicating with others, especially while in a position of leadership. But there are often barriers that impede successful transmission and comprehension, resulting from any number of factors. To ensure effective communication, you need to be cognizant of these barriers.

Barriers to Communication

1. *Language:* Use of overly technical terms or jargon that the other party is unfamiliar with can lead to misunderstandings. Ambiguity, lack of clarity and cohesiveness, and disjointed talking points can leave the recipient confused. With a diverse workforce, there are more people whose native language is will not match your own, which can be further complicated by dialect and inflection.

2. *Mixed Signals:* This occurs when nonverbal communication is inconsistent with what is being conveyed verbally. While delivering a message, body language, eye contact, posture, and demeanor are signals received by the listener. These signals, however subtle, can distort the perception of what is being communicated. The core of understanding is often based on the nonverbal aspect of communication.

3. *Mindset:* Attitude, bias, and preconceived notions all affect communication. Due to interpersonal issues, opposing views, resistance to change, or past experiences, an individual may be resistant to receiving a particular message, employing inattentiveness or intentional misinterpretation to distort and disregard a message. The same holds true if the individual transmitting the message has a similar attitude, compromising open and objective discourse.

4. *Emotions:* If someone is angry, resentful, or has had a negative previous encounter with the individual or

organization delivering a message, he or she may be resistant to receiving that message clearly. If there is a failure to believe in the basic underpinnings of what is being conveyed, this lack of buy-in results in further pushback. Emotional quotient plays a significant role in this process if the individual transmitting the message has been unable to establish any connection with the audience. Someone with a poor self-image or a lack of confidence will find it difficult to articulate points convincingly, to express a clear viewpoint in a timely fashion, or to engage successfully in teamwork and cooperation.

5. *Assumptions:* It is natural for someone to make certain assumptions regarding their audience or the message prior to an interaction. However, those assumptions need to reviewed and assessed. The individual or audience the message is being conveyed to may not be prepared to grasp the basic concepts. Conversely, the person conveying the message may not have the proper background or knowledge to convey the information clearly. The sender may think the message is important to the receiver when it is not. This can happen in business-to-customer meetings, where presentations are made based on what the presenter assumes is of importance to the customer, when, in reality, it may hold no value and provide no differentiation from something they already have. Meetings or conversations may also end with one party wholly misunderstanding what was communicated,

leaving the other party with the misconception that the message was transmitted successfully.

6. *Culture:* The world is shrinking. It is necessary to be able to interact across geographic lines with the global business community. Business practices and social customs can vary greatly depending upon geography, and differences sometimes present a substantial barrier. If not understood and addressed properly, miscommunication and misunderstandings will assuredly transpire and hinder the ability to develop a relationship. Cross-cultural communication encompasses a number of areas, including language, how one greets an individual, how questions are asked, the concept of personal space, body language, and even minutiae such as how to pour a drink at dinner.

7. *Gender:* There is an inherent difference in communication styles between genders. While this difference is not as vast as it used to be, it is nevertheless essential to understand and address, especially as gender heterogeneity is now the norm in the West, and increasingly globally. It is not uncommon for men and women to misunderstand each other owing to different communication styles. For example, women have a higher emotional quotient than men, which is not conjecture but an established fact. There are differences in communication style, conflict resolution, and relationship building. These differences can be exacerbated by

outdated stereotyping or companies with workforces disproportionately consisting of one gender.

8. *Physical:* Distance between people, offices, or organizations, even closed doors, are examples of physical barriers that restrict communication. A noisy and distracting environment, a poorly laid-out conference room lacking adequate sight lines, or poorly designed office space can also act as barriers, along with poor acoustics and subpar audiovisual equipment. Quiet talkers combined with a robust HVAC system can be a lethal combination.

9. *Technology:* While technology has been a boon for communication, it can also be an impediment. If someone is texting or looking at their phone in the middle of a conversation or meeting, chances are they will retain little of what is being said. The same holds true of laptops, where individuals can spend time on whatever may be of interest to them, perhaps preparing to find data buttressing their next conversation, all the while paying little attention to, and comprehending less of, what is currently being communicated.

10. *Timing:* While this last barrier may not be obvious, communicating something at the wrong time will have a detrimental effect on both your ability to deliver a message and on another party's ability to receive the message. If prevailing circumstances are a distraction, the message will not be properly received. If an individual is taken unawares or given short notice of

a subject requiring more discussion, the message may provoke an emotional response, negatively affecting message integrity.

Good communication is essential as you set out to seek your career, and there is always the possibility for improvement. Improving communication skills requires a comprehensive approach, focusing on the following areas:

Improving Your Communication

1. *Listen:* Listening, of course, is an important part of communication. The better you listen, the better you communicate. If you don't clearly grasp what the other party is saying, it will be difficult to respond appropriately or to follow up with the right questions. Listening requires focus, concentration, and active engagement with others. Making it obvious that you are giving the listener your undivided attention helps establish a rapport and demonstrates respect for the other party, which will not go unnoticed. Conversely, checking your phone or computer during a conversation conveys a lack of attention, damaging your rapport with the speaker. Do not sit there letting your mind wander or think only about what you want to say next, as you may miss key points in the conversation. Avoid interrupting others or finishing their sentences by paraphrasing. When responding, always think before you speak.

2. *Learn Nonverbal Communication:* A person's opinion of you is formed within thirty seconds of meeting you, based on your demeanor and outward appearance. Making eye contact, smiling, being cordial, showing confidence but not arrogance, and being approachable will go a long way toward someone forming a positive opinion of you and, consequently, being more receptive to your input. While in conversation, be sure to maintain eye contact and good posture, be attentive, and speak in a natural and even tone, clearly pronouncing your words. Your facial expressions and demeanor should match, reinforcing the message and imbuing trust. If you are saying one thing, but your facial expressions and body language say another, you lose credibility. Closely observe the signals you receive from the other party, as well. If they are inattentive, not maintaining eye contact, and sitting with their legs and arms crossed, they are not being receptive to your message. Pay attention to the totality of the signals—don't focus on one gesture or signal in particular—and trust your intuition.

3. *Study:* Learn the techniques and subtleties of different types of communication, focusing on those areas in which you have shortcomings. There are various ways to do this. Read books on writing and presentation skills. You can also take courses on communication online, in person, or through a workshop. If you want to improve your public-speaking skills, join a public-speaking group such as Toastmasters. Reading is also

a good way to expand your vocabulary. Reading books and journals specific to your interest makes you more familiar with the language, terminology, and jargon. Study videos of people you admire giving presentations. Likewise, you can record yourself giving a speech or a presentation, giving you a clear picture of others will see you and allowing you to identify weaknesses in your performance. Role-playing with others to simulate discussions or situations is an excellent way to shore up your response and increase your confidence.

4. *Confidence:* Being confident and in control will improve your effectiveness in communicating and connecting with others. It is difficult to properly communicate when you are anxious or overly emotional—you struggle to think clearly, you make mistakes, and you lose your composure. You may lack confidence in certain settings due to inexperience, lack of competence, or simply not understanding how you should conduct yourself. Increasing your proficiency, striving to learn as much as possible, believing in yourself, and being seen as an expert in your chosen field will do wonders for your confidence, so put in the time. Recognize the settings that trigger anxiety and insecurity. Practice at home or with others, simulating those circumstances. Develop strategies and coping techniques, like visualization, which enable you to maintain your composure. Put yourself out there; insert yourself into those situations you find most uncomfortable. With time and practice,

much of this will become second nature. While practice may not make you perfect, it will make you better and more confident.

5. *Clarity:* Think about what you are communicating, explain why it is important, and convey it in the most simple and straightforward manner possible. In today's world, where people are inundated with hundreds of messages per day, clarity and conciseness are valued highly. If a more formal document or format is required, put together an outline, and break it down into key points. The points must be in a logical order that flows, enabling the reader to quickly grasp the information. If the subject is complex, make it simple; break it down into smaller, more readily understood pieces using bullet points. Visual aids and graphs can be extremely effective at condensing complex information into an easily understood graphic. Review your written work, rereading it a few times to yourself and out loud. Check your spelling and grammar; tighten it up, and stay on message.

6. *Venue:* Many default to the mode of communication they are most comfortable with, which may not always be the most appropriate medium. There are times when some messages are more effectively conveyed orally, and there are times when it is best written. Oral communication can be challenging when the audience is dispersed geographically. Another factor is audience size—the more people involved, the more difficult it is

to communicate, especially complex topics. Use your judgment in these situations. The larger the audience, the more straightforward and concise the message needs to be to avoid widespread misunderstanding.

7. *Awareness:* Know your audience; put yourself in their shoes. What is their background, what is important to them, and what is their basic understanding of what you are conveying? Avoid making assumptions, and match your message and your delivery to the audience. Anticipate their objections and concerns, and have clear responses prepared in advance. Consider cultural differences, understanding that social norms vary greatly. If language is a barrier, speak in a slower, even-toned manner, avoiding jargon or slang. If necessary, use an interpreter to bridge the language barrier.

8. *Feedback:* Engage with the other party or audience to ensure that you are understood. Get feedback by asking questions, which demonstrates your interest in understanding your audience. This opens a dialogue instead of letting the conversation shut down. If some of the feedback is not to your liking, take it professionally, not personally. Respect the other party's point of view—do not get defensive; empathize with others, and ensure that you get as much feedback as possible to confirm that you got your message across.

9. *Assertiveness:* Being assertive does not mean being aggressive. It means being assured and confident enough to

express your opinion. Many people with social anxiety have difficulty in expressing their views, taking a passive role both socially and professionally. When you have an opinion about something, having thought it through first, take the initiative, and speak up. You don't have to agree to everything, and it isn't impolite to say "No."

10. *Regimen:* Being a good communicator is an ongoing endeavor requiring commitment, discipline, and good habits. Treat communication just like any other skill, and develop it. Be cognizant of shortfalls you have in certain areas, make it a point to improve, and come up with a plan.

Email

Nothing has changed the way we communicate more than electronic communication. The invention of the telegraph in the nineteenth century resulted in the ability to communicate long distances via wireless telegraphy. The first widespread use occurred during the American Civil War, when it proved to be a valuable means of rapid communication and coordination. General McClellan used the telegraph to his advantage on numerous occasions and is credited with having the first teleconference by telegraphing with various field commanders simultaneously. President Abraham Lincoln used it as his primary means of communication with his field commanders. President Lincoln spent countless hours in the telegraph room of the Department of War building, a short walk behind the White House, where he would receive updates and give orders.

Technology evolved rapidly over the ensuing decades, with electronic mail first available in 1971. Since then, largely due to personal computers and mobile phones, it has grown to the point where electronic mail, or email, is the predominant form of communication worldwide, particularly in the workplace, with more than 90% of all mail being sent or received electronically. Each day, there are 269 billion emails worldwide, generated from 4.3 billion users, which results in a worldwide total of 74 trillion emails each year.

We can now communicate in milliseconds with someone across the country or halfway around the world. We are never more than a click away from sending or receiving an email or a message, the omnipresent personal computer or mobile phone being your instant gateway. What was initially meant to allow us more freedom to live and work independently has resulted in us never being "away from our desk," as we are constantly tethered to these devices.

Speed and volume have their benefits but also their drawbacks. Bombarded by hundreds of emails and messages per day, we see a constant flow of information, most often with speed trumping style, resulting in short fragments of information lacking context. Constant communication does not always equate to good communication, with multitasking resulting in abbreviated attention spans as we continually check and respond to emails and messages.

The first thing to do is to avoid getting on the electronic treadmill. You must manage this aspect of your communication habits. As you enter the workforce, develop a regimen that makes the best use of your time to become more efficient and effective, and implement the following measures:

Communicating More Effectively via Electronic Mail

1. Set aside times each day for checking and responding to emails versus checking continually.

2. Read the entire email instead of skimming over it, responding to it, or forwarding it to others. Responding without adequate review or comprehension can create miscommunication and confusion. When reading on a mobile device, such as a smartphone, take special care since the screen format creates visual limitations.

3. Clarity, conciseness, and brevity are important when crafting or responding to email. Try to say more with less, enabling receiving parties to quickly grasp key elements of your message. Use shorter sentences and bullet points so that your receiver can quickly glean and understand what you want to convey.

4. Proofread email for grammar, and reread it before you send it. Consider if you even need to send it in the first place.

5. Consider the addresses on your email, especially when responding to a message. Will your email be received by one person or several? Simply sending something to a wider audience is not always effective communication.

6. Avoid hasty, emotional responses you'll later regret. Once you click, it's gone, and it can quickly become viral if others decide to forward it to additional parties. The same holds true for social media. Be cognizant of your digital footprint.

7. Do not use email for debating or arguing a position, especially with a wide audience.

8. Consider the appropriateness of the subject matter before sending your message. Something which is confidential, private in nature, or sensitive should normally not be sent into cyberspace. Keep subject matter work-related, and avoid discussing political or social issues. Chances are your email at work is being monitored, which is an additional reason for proper content and tone. Due to time and distance considerations, there may be instances when it is operationally necessary to broach sensitive matters via email. When deemed necessary, limit the number of addressees, and ensure that transmission is as secure as possible.

9. Keep a written list next to your desk. Taking the time to write to-do items down will help reinforce your short-term memory and enable you to get away from your computer screen.

10. Follow guidelines for use of email within your organization.

Communication is a skill that can be learned and developed. It is one of the skills companies look for most when hiring and promoting. Being an effective communicator is a prerequisite for success in all aspects of your life. Remember the following:

1. *Types of Communication:* Understand the three types of communication.

2. *Barriers:* Develop an awareness of the barriers to communication, including nonverbal communication.

3. *Plan:* Develop a plan to improve your communication in all three areas; eliminate the barriers to communication and practice.

4. *Email:* Use it properly, effectively, and appropriately.

5. *Priority:* Make it a priority to master the art of communication, adopting a regimen that reinforces good communication practices.

Leadership

"Leadership is an action, not a position."

Are leaders born, or are they made? There has been a great deal of research and debate on this subject. Some hold that leaders are born, others that they are made.

Leadership is more of a developed skill than something you are born with. If it were simply inborn, any further discussion of this subject would be pointless. Yes, some people are born with characteristics or traits that predispose them to become leaders. However, for the majority of us, if we want to develop our leadership skills, it is eminently doable as long as we are open-minded, we listen, accept feedback, and continually work on improvement.

Dwight D. Eisenhower described leadership as "the art of getting someone else to do something you want done because they want to do it." Put another way, it is "leading a group of people in a cohesive and effective manner to accomplish a specific purpose." While it may sound easy in theory, leadership is a challenge in practice. There is often an assumption that just because someone is in a management position or is leading a team, he or she is providing leadership, when, in fact, this may not be the case. An ineffective leader will find it difficult to actually lead anybody and will likely be doing more harm than good. And more often than not, ineffective leadership is not recognized until it is too late.

It is essential to grasp the difference between positional authority and personal authority. Being in a position of authority is not equivalent to being an effective leader. If a person in authority leads principally by virtue of his or her position and lacks the skills required to provide effective leadership, morale and performance will be compromised, and results will suffer. Consequently, before someone is put into a position of leadership, it is important to make an assessment of the individual's leadership skills. When evaluating a candidate, trust your instinct or intuition. People are naturally drawn to someone who can communicate and inspire them, who has a positive demeanor, and who gets results.

A leader must be secure enough to bring good people with the best talent possible onboard while also being sensitive to the chemistry of the team. The leader should trust the team and give them room to maneuver—empowering them, but also holding them accountable. There should be clear goals in place, with metrics to measure progress. As events conspire to create obstacles, as they inevitably do, a good leader should be proactive and innovative in guiding the team to find solutions.

In times of adversity, a good leader must be levelheaded and inspire confidence.

Throughout this process, individuals will be identified who can step in and take over in the event of a vacancy or if a personnel change is required. And due to the diversity and globalization of today's workforce, someone in a leadership position will be dealing with individuals of various backgrounds and cultures. Effective two-way communication is essential to finding the right person for the job.

Every company should offer leadership training or development, and, while many do, some do not, merely giving it lip service. If an individual does not have ready access to any company training program, there are other venues available. Leadership requires a set of skills that can be developed if we are willing to invest the time and effort. It is a continuum, and we are always learning and developing. These are the five character traits of an effective leader:

Characteristics of Effective Leadership

1. *Communication:* A leader is proficient in all facets of communication. Whether it be one-on-one or in a group, leaders are able to articulate their vision in a clear manner so that everyone understands the strategy and their role. A leader is approachable and confident in approaching others. Understanding and effectively utilizing nonverbal communication conveys openness, enabling effective two-way communication and feedback. Leaders get out from behind the desk and make

it a point to converse with employees in all matters, business or otherwise.

2. *Inspiration:* Leaders set the tone and provide inspiration and motivation. They are energetic, engaging, and self-assured. They face difficult issues or challenges with a can-do attitude. Leaders have the discipline and determination to see things through and remain focused throughout an ordeal. They lead by example and do not presume to follow a different set of rules than others. Their strong belief, passion, and ability to articulate their vision directly affects those around them, instilling belief in the cause and confidence in the mission.

3. *Integrity:* A leader's character is beyond reproach, characterized by behavior that is ethical, respectful, and honest at all times. A leader exhibits a high degree of transparency. When commitments are made, they are honored. Leaders do not stray from their value system when convenient or when faced with adversity. A leader is self-assured but has the humility and grace to admit mistakes and move on. When mistakes are made, the emphasis is on finding solutions, not casting blame. Integrity builds credibility and trust among the team, which enhances loyalty and cooperation.

4. *Team Development:* A leader understands that it is teams working together toward a common goal that determines success. The leader must assemble the right people,

considering strengths and weaknesses, and nurturing that all-important quality of effective teams—chemistry. The team members should not be mirror images of the leader but should augment those areas where the leader has shortcomings. There should be clarity about the goals and each team member's role. The leader should be familiar with the principles and processes involved in the plan and should have confidence in the team members, trusting them and delegating responsibility, empowering them to perform. When problems occur, a leader provides direction, assisting in prioritization and planning. A leader is decisive, with an understanding of the decision-making process. It is one thing to make a decision; it is another to articulate the reasons for the decision in a confident, self-assured manner.

5. *Adaptability:* A leader is able to adapt to changing or unforeseen circumstances, handling the ambiguity, uncertainty, and conflict in a graceful and self-assured manner. Adaptability requires different ways of thinking, creativity, and open-mindedness. Avoid focusing on only one approach or strategy, as the world is constantly changing. Recognizing those changes and being able to adapt and make the correct decisions imbues confidence in the leader among the team. Effective leaders are also able to vary their management style, depending upon the circumstances and personnel involved, as there is no "one-size-fits-all" leadership style across the spectrum.

"Leadership style" refers to the behavior of the leader and how planning, direction, and decision-making are accomplished with the team. Leadership style should not be confused with a personality trait. There is a distinction between the two, and an interrelationship, as the traits resident within an individual affect management style and adaptability to an extent. Everyone has a primary leadership style. The effective leader recognizes this but is also able to pivot and change styles as different scenarios and circumstances demand. The following are the three basic leadership styles. Each style has its place, with concordant advantages and disadvantages.

Basic Leadership Styles

1. *Autocratic:* This style of leadership is positional in nature, with the leader being authoritative. The autocratic leader is the dominant voice and decision maker. Orders are given and expected to be followed, with little to no input from the team. This type of leadership style is appropriate in times of crisis, when there is little time for deliberation and decisions must be quick. The benefits of this style are fast decision-making, reduced risk of misunderstanding, as there is no filter, and rapid response focused solely on the mission. However, this approach limits creativity and input from the team, which, over the long term, is demoralizing and demotivating. A good leader who can perform in circumstances like these, which are time-sensitive and critical in nature, is appreciated by the team for leading them through a

crisis. This authoritarian style of leadership should be used sparingly, and in today's environment, it is not a style that is successful on an ongoing basis.

2. *Participative:* Another term for this leadership style is "democratic." Although the leader is still the ultimate decision-maker, this style is a mixture of positional authority and personal authority, with emphasis on the latter. A participative leader values input from team members, encouraging a free exchange of information and ideas. The leader's goal is to achieve consensus through participation, so when a decision has been made, everyone has had a chance to voice their opinion. The benefit of this approach is that each team member feels part of the decision and contributes to this process, which, in turn, boosts morale and helps foster buy-in. Enabling others to have their voices heard can help gain different perspectives as well as a better understanding of the issues and options, since the knowledge and expertise of the team is more effectively utilized.

3. *Laissez-faire:* Other terms associated with this style are "delegative" or "hands-off." Team members are assigned tasks or projects and left to their own devices to complete them, with the leader providing support when needed. The leader has faith and confidence in the team, affording them a high degree of freedom and autonomy. This approach works best when employees are self-motivated, highly skilled and proficient in their field, and able to manage their time effectively. In this

situation, however, if the proficiency and effectiveness of a team member is less than envisioned, the quality of the work may suffer, and deadlines may be missed. There is a time and place for this style; do not be hesitant to use it, but match the right people to the task, ensuring that they have the proficiency and drive to get it done.

The preferred approach is one that balances a concern for the employees with the task at hand. A good leader understands there is no best style that fits all situations and has the awareness to adapt a style based on the circumstances and makeup of the team, shifting gears when necessary. Most leadership training focuses on what to do, but you also need to be aware of what *not* to do. Here are the most common leadership mistakes:

Leadership Mistakes

1. *Mismatch:* Specific expertise or achievement in one area does not necessarily translate into leadership-role success. For example, just because someone has excelled at sales does not guarantee sales-management success. The necessary leadership qualities may not be resident within that individual, and there may not have been adequate training or development for the individual prior to the promotion. It may be a disservice to the company and the individual to assign someone without leadership qualities to a leadership role. Prior to stepping into a leadership role, the candidate's capacity for leadership

should be candidly assessed by both the organization and the individual being considered.

2. *Confusing Positional with Personal Authority:* Having a title does not make someone a leader. The largest determinant of success is the character of the person in the position. Someone who relies on position or title to wield influence and give orders, but lacks the necessary traits and exhibits a poor leadership style, will lose the respect of the team and cause performance to suffer.

3. *Improper Delegation:* Delegating implies that the leader has confidence in the individual to whom the task has been assigned. It involves giving up a degree of control, shifting the emphasis from managing an activity to leading an individual. Good leaders must be comfortable with this approach and understand that their role is to provide the necessary direction and support. A good balance needs to be struck to avoid micromanaging, while at the same time not being too hands-off.

4. *Not Listening:* A leader needs to be accessible, with open channels of communication. A leader should also spend more time listening than speaking. This feedback is important since it provides a clear picture of the progress and needs of the team. The leader should make it a point to listen actively and ask questions. An open-door policy and a participative, transparent leadership style foster an environment that enhances two-way communication.

5. *Lack of Definition:* The leader should make it clear what the goals are and what success looks like. Clarity of purpose and direction, with each team member understanding his or her role, helps avoid mistakes and misunderstandings. When circumstances change, the leader should be transparent and convey the information to the team to avoid surprises later. Information is a management tool, not a weapon.

6. *Lack of Development:* An effective leader is focused not only on the mission but also on people. The leader makes it a priority to improve the skill sets and competency of the team by providing coaching and guidance. It will be necessary to provide feedback, even constructive criticism, as part of this development. Taking an interest in the development of the team engenders trust, respect, and loyalty, which results in higher productivity and lower employee turnover.

7. *Not Being Proactive:* A good leader needs to be situationally aware of inevitable and constant change. The leader will have to anticipate changes or problems that arise and be prepared to face them—and sooner rather than later. Planning ahead and anticipating, versus waiting and reacting, will result in less disruption to progress.

8. *Avoiding Conflict:* One of the most difficult adjustments for a new leader is the ability to handle conflict. Avoidance is not a good strategy, since issues being avoided tend not to go away on their own. They fester

and resurface at a later date, often resulting in a minor issue becoming a major problem. Many of these issues will be employee-related and will require intervention by the leader. A leader needs to be fair and impartial, to be willing to make decisions, and to understand that it is not possible to please everyone.

9. *Confusing Friendship with Business:* While everyone wants to be liked, in this regard, it is more important that the leader be respected. There is an emotional quotient to leadership. The leader should get to know the team, while being cognizant of the dynamics at play. A leader should strike the right balance. If the pendulum swings too far toward personal friendship, it could jeopardize the objectivity of the leader when faced with tough decisions in the future.

10. *Not Setting an Example:* Leadership is done by example. A leader is not held to a different standard, but to a higher standard—not living by one set of rules while expecting others to abide by a different set. A leader's behavior should be above reproach, adhering to a strong work ethic, with uncompromised integrity and dignity. The leader should be humble, giving credit where credit is due, accepting accountability for mistakes versus casting aspersions elsewhere. A commitment made is a commitment honored. Decisions are made in an even-handed, objective manner, devoid of negative emotions and ranting.

"Leadership and learning are indispensable to each other," John F. Kennedy once observed. When, at some point in your career, you find yourself in a position of leadership—whether as an entrepreneur, manager, or team leader—it is important to remember that it is always possible to develop leadership skills and improve on them. To do this requires the following:

Developing Your Leadership

1. *Determine Your Style:* You need to determine your primary leadership style and identify its strengths and weaknesses. Conducting a self-assessment and an online leadership-skills analysis is a good first step. You can go further and enlist the assistance of a leadership coach as well. Pay attention to how your style and competencies match up with your chosen career path.

2. *Learn:* Once you determine your leadership style, examine and understand your strengths and weaknesses. Leverage your strengths by pursuing opportunities in areas where you are strongest. Do not try to be something you are not. Acknowledging your weaknesses and taking the necessary measures to overcome them will further improve your effectiveness. Online leadership-development courses, seminars, coaches, and organizations that specialize in leadership development are all available options. Develop a plan with goals and metrics, making continuous improvement a priority.

3. *Communication:* Master the ability to communicate verbally and nonverbally, and practice active listening. Be cognizant of the barriers to communication, understanding how to appropriately communicate based on the situation or individual. Be direct in order to avoid ambiguity and uncertainty, and to prevent misdirecting your energy. Nurture an atmosphere that fosters two-way communication, welcoming feedback and taking constructive criticism in stride.

4. *Planning:* Define the vision and goals for the team or company. Invest the time to develop a plan with metrics and timelines, ensuring that everyone has a clear understanding of their role. Meetings should have a clear agenda, with everyone having a common understanding of what is agreed to. See the bigger picture, maintain situational awareness, and be proactive. The plan needs to be crisply executed, with decisions made in a timely manner along the way.

5. *Delegate:* Learn to let go and trust people. There is a difference between directing and leading. Be a leader. Do not be afraid to delegate—you can't do everything. Individuals responsible for specific tasks or projects should be given the authority and resources to succeed with your support and should be held accountable for any results.

6. *Initiative:* Do not be content to limit the tasks you undertake to those tasks at hand. If there is an area

or an issue where you believe you have a unique skill set or ability to contribute and make a difference, take the initiative and volunteer. Being involved in projects outside your scope of interest broadens your horizons and gets you out of your comfort zone. "Gung-ho" is derived from a Chinese phrase meaning "work together." Being gung-ho and exhibiting a willingness to take on new responsibility shows enthusiasm and sets you apart.

7. *Inspire:* Nothing great gets accomplished without passion. Having a firm belief in what you are doing, and being passionate and enthusiastic, will have a halo effect. Your behavior will be a source of motivation to others. If a team member is having trouble or hits a rough patch, take the time to talk with him or her. Sometimes it just takes someone listening to raise spirits.

8. *Set the Example:* Be a role model by setting an example and showing the team you adhere to the same standards you expect of others. Be disciplined and consistent in your processes, show up to work and meetings on time, and demonstrate your competence and willingness to learn. Maintain a positive attitude and avoid negative conversations or comments regarding personnel or the company. When faced with adversity, rise to the occasion, and remain centered and in control. When faced with failure, accept accountability, learn from it, and move on. When realizing success, exhibit humility, and give credit where it is due.

9. *Treat Everyone With Dignity and Respect:* Treat everyone as you would want to be treated. Understand that your team members are not simply cogs in a machine but are individuals with their own unique set of characteristics and abilities. Get to know your team, and remember that they have lives outside of work, with families and people who depend on them. Respect them for who they are and what they do. Exhibit a genuine interest in their well-being, and always have their back.

10. *Seek the Truth:* In this age of multiple avenues for instantaneous communication, words can travel faster than the truth. When faced with an issue, whether business- or personnel-related, ensure that you have all the facts and that the information is credible. Avoid rushing to judgment, which only compounds the trouble caused by decisions based on misleading or faulty intelligence. Say what you will do, and do what you say, always honoring your commitments—your word is your bond.

Leadership is a skill you can develop, just as with anything else. Keep the following points in mind in order to develop as a leader:

1. *Acknowledge* your strengths and weaknesses, and develop a plan.

2. *Commit* to exercising those traits inherent in effective leaders.

3. *Learn* as much as you can about leadership principles and techniques.

4. *Practice:* Put theory into practice; be resolute; do not compromise.

5. *Set an Example:* Have the courage, discipline, and resilience to be an exemplary leader at all times.

PART THREE

Persevere and Adapt—
Never, Ever Give Up

"Winners are not people who never fail,
but people who never quit."

CHAPTER ONE

Adversity

"Not all storms come to disrupt your life.
Some come to clear the path."

"That which does not kill you will make you stronger," quoted German philosopher Friedrich Nietzsche. At first glance, this statement seems to declare that hardship or trauma builds strength. However, what Nietzsche means by this is that it is not the pain itself, but the experience of withstanding or overcoming the adversity that makes you stronger. Simply because you have gone bankrupt does not mean you are stronger or more prepared to deal with adversity. If, however, you have successfully dealt with the experience and moved on, then you are better equipped to handle future adverse circumstances.

All of us will face some degree of adversity in our lives; this is inevitable. You can't run from it. You can't hide from it. You have to deal with it—embrace it as a learning experience, accept responsibility, take action, and move on. The true test of character is not how you behave when things are going well, but how you respond when things don't work out and events seem to conspire against you. Adversity will help you grow. It will make you stronger. As President John F. Kennedy said, "Turn scars into stars."

Adversity comes in many forms, often financial, emotional, or health related. These events can be brief and have a limited effect, or they can have a profound and prolonged effect on your life. Losing your smartphone is not an adverse event— it is an inconvenience. Being unable to make payments on your home, car, or phone because you have lost your job and are struggling to find a new one qualifies as adversity. These experiences can be valuable life lessons if we learn from them and learn to avoid them. Some of these circumstances will be beyond your control, and others will be self-inflicted due to poor decisions, lack of oversight, or arrogance. Your character is defined not by what you *go through* but how you *get through it*. Successful people do not give up when faced with adversity. They have the resilience, strength of character, and courage to "Find a way or make one," as General Hannibal famously directed his officers when faced with the daunting task of crossing the Pyrenees, elephants and all.

When faced with adverse circumstances, many of the points in this book come into play. If you are committed to what you are doing, your strong belief and faith in your mission will help you stay the course. If you have conditioned yourself, both mentally and physically, you are better able to deal with the stress and uncertainty. If your personal life is in order, this provides a further buttress, as negative circumstances in one aspect of your life can spill over into others.

The sum total of these ups and downs—and here we focus on the downs—shapes you as an individual and determines your ability to successfully rebound. While it may not seem so at the time, these trials offer you valuable knowledge. They help develop resiliency, a key trait in being able to effectively deal with adversity. Such experiences also afford the opportunity to develop in ways you may not have been able to otherwise. As you encounter adverse circumstances, keep the following five points in mind:

Benefits of Adversity

1. *Increases Experience:* You need to be tested or challenged in order to learn and grow. Every adverse circumstance overcome is a lesson learned that helps you grow and develop your capacity to deal with future occurrences. If you have never experienced something in your life, it is difficult to anticipate how you would react to it. Adversity may also reveal the character of those around you as you witness how they respond.

2. *Presents Challenges:* Adversity will challenge you in new ways, resulting in experiences you otherwise would not have encountered. These challenges help you develop as you strive to make the most of a bad situation and turn things around. Facing these challenges head on, coping with them, and developing a recovery strategy embolden you and give you confidence.

3. *Builds Resiliency:* These experiences develop your capacity to maintain resolve and determination through tough times. Stress and anxiety are twin components, affecting everyone dealing with adversity. Being able to effectively cope with the stressors associated with adversity enables you to cultivate a range of skills, making you stronger, better equipped, and more resilient.

4. *Imparts Perspective:* Times of adversity make us more greatly appreciate when things go smoothly. You will take satisfaction from the fact that you survived it and from the knowledge that adversity is only temporary. You will also adopt a state of mind that accepts adversity as inevitable and conquerable, knowing you survived once and will do so again—a positive mindset that will serve you well in the future.

5. *Improves Planning:* What you have learned about yourself and those around you can be the basis for well-developed alternatives and contingency plans that can be quickly and confidently executed during the next adverse event.

When adversity strikes, your mindset is your primary weapon. It is how you react, how you decide to respond, and what you do that determine your ability to overcome the obstacles you face. As you face these inevitable challenges, adhere to the following steps:

Dealing with Adversity

1. *Accept:* The first thing is to accept what has happened; what's done is done. You will learn from this experience, but, for now, you must look for ways to solve the problem. Focus on finding solutions instead of excuses. Accept responsibility instead of casting blame. Face the challenge head-on; view it as an opportunity rather than an obstacle. Move forward, understanding that every problem has a solution.

2. *Understand:* Get the facts. Often, problems are compounded by inaccurate information or misunderstandings. Before any action, ensure you get as complete an understanding as possible of what went wrong and why. Ask questions instead of making assumptions, drilling down to the basic issues and underlying causes of this predicament. Once you have defined the problem, determine which factors are in your control and which factors are not in your control. Determine what choices you have and what resources to use, focusing on what you can do, versus what you cannot.

3. *Respond:* You want to avoid a knee-jerk reaction and, at the same time, launch an initial response to the crisis. Focus on what steps you can take in the short-term, however small, to exhibit movement and to show that action is being taken. These initial actions will provide reassurance that you are in charge and on top of things.

While you may not be completely on top of things at this point—and likely you are not—perception is reality. A strong initial statement setting the right tone will help assuage fear and have a calming effect.

4. *Composure:* As a leader, you want to project a confident and calm demeanor, regardless of the circumstances. If the team sees that you are unfazed, they will find comfort in your example. Conversely, if they see you emotional and agitated, their imagination will run wild, assuming the worst. Set the tone by reinforcing your commitment and belief in the cause. "Strength and honor" is a phrase made famous by Maximus Decimus Meridius in the movie *Gladiator.* Your mantra should be "strength and confidence."

5. *Mindset:* You are defined not by the crisis but by how you deal with it. Your mindset will play a key role in how things turn out. A confident demeanor and a positive attitude, laced with enthusiasm, are contagious. Exhibit a can-do attitude, focusing on what can be done, instead of anticipating the worst. Most of those around you will embrace this perspective, but not all. Pay close attention to the doom-and-gloomers among the team. Their negativity can have an insidious effect on morale and can compromise your mission.

6. *Strengths:* During a crisis is not the time to launch a self-improvement program. Focus on your strengths and what you do best. This also holds true for the team

around you. By concentrating on your strengths with the best people, you will realize quicker progress and boost morale. You will have to place your faith in your team to see how they perform. Trust your instincts, and trust your team. The added responsibility may have a galvanizing effect as they rise to the occasion.

7. *Seek Help:* What you are going through is not unique. It may be unique to you and those around you, but it has happened before, in some way, shape, or form. If you or anyone else on your team has not had to deal with a crisis of this nature, seeking outside help from someone who has can be a valuable aid to your recovery. This individual can give you a different perspective, and it's helpful to get a different set of eyes looking at a problem. Do not hesitate to ask for help, and don't view such a request as a sign of weakness. If you do seek outside help, make sure the individual or entity is qualified by checking their credentials and experience. Ensure they have the requisite interpersonal skills essential to fostering open communication.

8. *Values:* When experiencing an adverse event, a compelling factor in effectively dealing with the crisis is unyielding faith and belief in one's purpose. This sense of conviction will provide a safeguard for you and the organization. Do not lose sight of what you strive to do and why you are doing it. Take every opportunity to emphasize your beliefs and core values, reinforcing your commitment. Now is not the time to take shortcuts or

to compromise, as the true test of character is revealed during these turbulent times.

9. *Plot a Course:* Once you have all the facts and have considered the options, develop a plan. Involve as many team members in the development as possible, since their participation results in greater commitment. Create a road map with objectives and timelines, ensuring clear assignment of responsibility. Communicate the plan to the team, and continually monitor progress, providing support and direction as needed. Understand that the circumstances that led to this situation likely didn't happen all at once; the turnaround will likewise take time. Be systematic and deliberate in carrying out this plan, paying special attention to the process, since it is a series of steps all properly executed that will enable you to emerge from this crisis. Throughout this process, if certain efforts do not work, do not be beholden to one approach. Be flexible and willing to make course adjustments. Celebrate the successes—even the small ones—as this energizes the team and improves morale as their progress and contributions are acknowledged.

10. *Team Health:* Some team members may not be as resilient or emotionally equipped to handle adverse circumstances. Some rise to the occasion, and some crumble; everyone handles adversity and the resultant stressors differently. To the best of your ability, do everything you can to maintain morale by setting an example. At the same time, keep a watchful eye on team members

who are showing signs of stress and are not handling the situation well. Keeping them in the line of fire will only make things worse, so adjustments in personnel assignments may be needed. If this is necessary, it should be done in a way that allows the individual's dignity and self-respect to remain intact. Bear in mind that, when things improve, this individual will continue to contribute; the current pace may be overwhelming for them. This should be handled in a tactful manner; tact may be easier said than done, but it is the hallmark of an effective leader.

Successful people and organizations will always face adversity, as life is not a continuous cycle of success and is not without its problems. When faced with adversity, find the inner strength to be courageous and resilient. Your attitude and mindset are central to overcoming the obstacle. Bear in mind that you have choices, so be fiercely determined to find a way—or make one—through your current challenge. There are always lessons to be learned. Accept this challenge as a learning opportunity, never give up, and commit yourself to developing understanding and insight, so that you do not find yourself in this same predicament again. When faced with adverse circumstances, keep the following points in mind:

1. *Accept:* Don't fight the problem—decide it. What is done is done.

2. *Understand:* Ask questions, get the facts, ensure information is accurate, and avoid making assumptions.

3. *Planning and Process:* Develop and implement a strategy, being rational and objective, and paying close attention to the requisite steps and timeline.

4. *Composure:* Project a calm, confident demeanor, with a positive mindset and attitude.

5. *Learn:* Take heed of why this happened and how you got through it, and vow not to let it happen again.

CHAPTER TWO

Failure

"With each failure, there is a lesson learned. It also shows you are trying. If you try, you risk failure. If you don't, you ensure it."

—Fred Stuvek Jr.

What is worse than failing? One answer is, "Never trying and never knowing." That is even worse than failure—to one day sit back, reflect, and wonder, "What if?" You may even regret your choice and think, "If I had it to do all over again, I would have given it a shot." The lesson here is to avoid making a decision for the wrong reasons, chief among them being the fear of failure. "There is only one way to avoid criticism: do nothing, say nothing, and be nothing." Those were Aristotle's comments concerning criticism. You can just as easily substitute the word "failure" for "criticism." The only way to avoid failure is to do nothing.

You need to be prepared to accept that failure is part of life. You are not alone in this regard, and you are not being singled out and tormented by the universe. If you are living your life and making decisions based on a fear of failure, you are doing yourself a great disservice.

No one likes to fail, some people can't handle it, and many go to great lengths, often at their own expense, to avoid it. But there is no way to avoid failure; life is a series of wins and losses, ups and downs. However, steps can be taken to reduce the number of failures and mitigate their impact. You can emerge wiser, stronger, and better equipped for the next challenge if you maintain the right mindset and take the right approach.

As Winston Churchill so eloquently pointed out, "Success is the ability to move from one failure to another with no loss of enthusiasm." With each failure, there are lessons to be learned. If the desired outcome is not achieved, take a close look at what went wrong. What could be done better or differently next time? Do not be afraid to get input from others, including team members and trusted advisors. Identify those factors that are in your control and those not in your control. Determine what you need to change next time. Also, take a look at what went right. Find ways to accentuate your strong points and further use them to your advantage.

Do not dwell on failure or languish in self-pity. Keep excuses to a minimum. Those in a leadership position should accept responsibility. Avoid the blame game—that is a nonstarter. Be positive and forthright; do not thwart constructive criticism. Encourage creative thinking and try to devise another way to approach the problem. When heading a team, try to develop consensus, but do not make it such an elaborate planning process that it becomes time consuming and inefficient. Have a contingency plan in place, as things do not always work out as planned.

History is replete with examples of individuals who had a vision and saw things through despite formidable obstacles. This is the norm, not the exception, since most success stories do not happen overnight and do not come easily. Abraham Lincoln ran for Congress twice and for the Senate twice, losing each time, and was elected president two years after his second failed bid for the Senate. Thomas Edison found hundreds of ways to fail at building a light bulb before succeeding. Henry Ford was bankrupt five times from previous business ventures before founding the Ford Motor Company. None of these individuals let failure define them, and they had a strong-enough belief in what they were doing to continue to move forward.

That is why it is so important to find something you believe in and are passionate about, and to associate yourself with successful people or organizations. It is this steadfast belief in yourself and your goals that will help you through downturns. If you are working with a solid group of people who are also firmly committed, everyone will pull together, craft a recovery strategy, improvise, adapt, and overcome.

You will assuredly be faced with adversity and experience failure, both professionally and personally. How one responds to these circumstances not only *reveals* character but also *builds* character. When faced with these difficult circumstances, there are several things one can do to weather the storm. If you pay attention to the recommendations throughout this book, you can get through just about anything, and you will be better off for it.

Success is several things done consistently well across the spectrum. Failure is the opposite, with the reasons for failure caused by any one or a combination of the following:

Reasons for Failure

1. *Staying in Your Comfort Zone:* We value winning above all else; many equate the thought of failing with losing. Consequently, a mindset of "never fail, never lose" sets in, which is a flawed way of thinking. You need to accept that failure is inevitable. The only way to avoid failure is to never try, which is itself a failure, in that you will never realize your potential. Your commitment to succeed must be stronger than your fear of failure. If you are going to be successful and stand out, you must avoid complacency. Put yourself out there. Be willing to accept failure, learn from it, and keep moving forward.

2. *Lack of Belief:* If you believe, you will achieve; if you don't, you won't. A passionate belief in what you are doing and confidence in your ability are essential. The absence of either one of these two ingredients will eventually sabotage you. Your strength of conviction will generate enthusiasm, which is contagious to those around you and will provide the grit necessary to weather the hard times. Your belief in yourself will imbue you with confidence to face whatever is put in front of you.

3. *Lack of Competence:* Your ability directly relates to your skill set, which should correlate to what you are doing. If

you do not have the necessary training or background, you will lack confidence, suffer from low self-esteem, and continually be on the defensive. Instead of finding ways to get something done, you'll devote your time to circumnavigating and avoiding situations. Being a poor communicator or lacking interpersonal skills can also play a role. Ensure that you are a good fit for what you are doing, play to your strengths, and develop a distinct set of competencies to enhance your prospects for continued success.

4. *Lack of Perseverance:* Nothing good comes easily or quickly. You must work for it and never give up. When we see someone who is successful, we must be aware that it did not happen overnight. We just see the success and overlook the setbacks, struggles, and failures the individual had to endure. Today, with society's inclination toward instant gratification, it is imperative for you to have the conviction, determination, and the will to win to weather the bad times and reach your goals.

5. *Lack of Character:* Character counts—it matters. Individuals with a negative attitude and fatalistic views do not imbue confidence. Those who spend more time arguing their position versus listening and learning do not work well with others. Holding others accountable but never accepting responsibility is unfair to those on the team. Intolerance and lack of empathy for those around you affect teamwork and morale. Holding others to one set of standards while compromising those

same standards through your actions undermines your personal authority.

6. *Lack of Discipline:* Discipline relates directly to self-control, which must be practiced in order to be disciplined. It means adhering to the highest standards of conduct and business practice, and avoiding shortcuts and temptations to do otherwise. Face problems head-on, and do not procrastinate. Stay the course as it pertains to your goals and your strategy; don't jump ship at the first sign of peril. You understand you have to put in the time, make sacrifices along the way, and exhibit a strong work ethic, setting an example for others.

7. *Lack of Focus:* From small rocks do avalanches begin. There needs to be continuing attention and focus on strategy, process, and implementation, including metrics and timelines. You need to be cognizant of direction, be on the lookout for warning signs, and make course adjustments when necessary. Avoid devoting an inordinate amount of time to distractions and activities, such as social media, that do not contribute to your personal and professional goals.

8. *Business Partners:* Most of the problems in business are people-related. It should come as no surprise that one of the most common causes of distress and failure in business is the result of selecting the wrong people for the team. This is especially true in smaller companies, where, due to control being shared by fewer individuals, the

effects of poor leadership and management are magnified, with narrower margins for error. Great care should be taken when putting together a team to ensure that you have the right balance of talent and good chemistry. It is just as important to make sure whomever you hire is who they say they are and has truly accomplished that which is being touted.

9. *Lack of Resources:* This is usually finance-related, pertaining either to the inability to raise funds or the depletion of funds. Raising capital is no small feat. One needs to go into this with realistic expectations, both in terms of money that can be raised and the length of time it will take. During a sustained operation, close attention needs to be paid to cash flow and trends, ensuring that reserves are set aside and, most importantly, that plans are realistic and attainable, not wildly or blithely developed.

10. *Poor Planning and Execution:* When a business is in peril or fails, poor planning and execution are always central contributors. An aggressive plan with bad management and poor execution is usually fatal. Miscommunication or lack of communication can also play a key role. Poor leadership combined with arrogance usually results in an inability, or even unwillingness, to accept feedback, which later manifests itself in an avalanche of hidden problems. A lack of clear goals and little to no accountability jeopardize your ability to track and determine progress toward objectives, metrics, and timelines.

The mettle of an organization and an individual's character are revealed in how they deal with failure. Avoidance is not a winning strategy. You must face failure head-on. When you find yourself in a predicament, adhere to these basic steps for your recovery:

When Dealing With Failure

1. *Mindset:* The first and most important thing to do when dealing with failure is to get your mind right. Without the right mindset and attitude, you will never be able to effectively deal and cope with failure. It will break you. Do not take it personally, and do not let it define you. It is not who you truly are. Do not dwell on it—it will not change what has happened. This is misdirected energy and only creates more angst. Accept that failure is inevitable and that anyone who has achieved something great has had their share of failures. You failed because you had the courage to try something and it did not work out, but you have a choice to make. That choice is how you choose to deal with it. Instead of feeling sorry for yourself and indulging in self-pity, look at this as a lesson on the path to success. Have faith in yourself, and know you are strong enough to find a way through it and smart enough to avoid the same mistake in the future. Do not lose sight of your greater purpose and your desire to attain your goal. The firm belief and commitment in what you are doing will provide the courage and wherewithal to keep moving forward. Maintain

your composure, stay focused, and stay positive. Avoid negativity, but at the same time accept constructive criticism. Maintain a sense of perspective and balance, ensuring that you take care of yourself. Adhere to your fitness regimen, as it will reduce the effect of some of your stressors and will help clear your head.

2. *Accurate Data and Feedback:* You need to find out what went wrong, what the consequences are, and what potential options exist. Basing your recovery and actions on inaccurate or misleading information compounds things, possibly turning a failure into a tragedy. It is imperative to get an accurate assessment, which requires candor and even brutal honesty. To do this, the environment must be conducive to this type of exchange of information. Now is not the time to cast blame, make excuses, or go into denial. The sole focus should be on understanding all the facts and circumstances and figuring a way to get out of the current predicament.

3. *Be Objective and Rational:* Exercise self-control, and resist actions or comments you will later regret. It is human nature to be emotional, even overwrought, in circumstances such as these. However, decisions made while in an emotional or angry state are almost always bad decisions, laden with negative consequences. They reflect well neither on the person nor on the entity, and, ultimately, they erode authority. Keep your head in the game. Comments and criticisms should be constructive in nature. You should review the information and data,

and process it carefully while avoiding rash or impulsive actions. If necessary, enlist a third party who has experience in dealing with similar situations; objective input could prove invaluable.

4. *Learn, Plan, and Adapt:* There are two lessons to be learned here. The first is to determine what caused the failure. The second is to take heed of the events causing the failure in order to prevent future recurrences. Understanding what caused the failure is essential to avoid repeating the same mistake. Break it down into the essential components. It often is not one thing but a series of events that caused it to happen. It could be related to strategy, execution, or human error—or all three, for that matter. Whatever the cause, get to the root of it, and take action. Determine what resources you have available and how much time you have. Once you have outlined a new plan of action and assessed the opportunities and risks, pay close attention to implementation and execution. Remember, this plan is the start of a long road ahead. If the plan is not proceeding as anticipated, find out why, adapt, and continue to move forward.

5. *Be Realistic and Resilient:* Emerging from failure is a process that will take time and will be fraught with ups and downs. It must be dealt with properly. Otherwise, it can have a detrimental impact on your life or your career. The factors that will determine what you can and can't do are usually resource- or time-related. Consequently,

you must be prepared to make tough decisions and accept consequences that may seem unpalatable. Remind yourself that anyone who wants to do anything of value will fail, and embrace this experience as a learning opportunity on your path to success. Pay heed not only to what went wrong but also to what went right, using this as a steppingstone along your path toward recovery. Perseverance and determination are critical. You must commit to having the character and strength of will to get through it. Take care of your people; there are others around you who may not be as resilient as you are and may not fare as well. Keep a watchful eye on them, doing your utmost to provide support, counsel, and leadership throughout the arduous road to recovery.

It took a number of factors to converge, over an extended period of time, to get into this predicament. Recovery will involve several steps over an extended period of time to extricate yourself or the organization from these dire circumstances. Keep the following points in mind:

1. *Acceptance:* You must accept failure for what it is—a learning experience and a consequence of taking action.

2. *Commitment:* Remember your commitment and your unyielding belief in what you are doing and what you are about.

3. *Mindset:* Get your mind right. Do not let this event define you; face it head-on with strength and confidence.

4. *Composure:* Keep your head in the game.

5. *Implement, Assess, and Adapt:* Develop a plan, continually assess progress, and make adjustments as required.

CHAPTER THREE

Team

"The bigger the dream, the more important the team."

While it would seem that having an outstanding product or service paired with an excellent strategy would be a sure-fire formula for success, there is another ingredient needed. If this ingredient is missing, the chances of success are seriously compromised. Depending upon the type of company and what stage the company is in, it could even jeopardize its survival. This essential ingredient is *the right team*. It sounds simple, but assembling the right team is one of the most difficult things to do and, arguably, the most important task a leader takes on.

All teams consist of a group of individuals. While the individuals may be highly skilled and capable, team success is predicated on how the individual capabilities of the team may be harnessed, enabling the team to function as a cohesive unit in the most effective and efficient manner possible. A group of the best and brightest people may be assembled, but if they fail to adequately interact, communicate, and cooperate, the results will be lackluster at best.

When looking at team candidates, there are several factors that must be considered. Two of the most important considerations are skills and EQ. There will be instances where an individual lacks the experience or technical know-how, but because they excel in other areas, they may be developed to grow into the position. For example, I once filled a fairly technical leadership position with someone who had no prior formal or hands-on experience in the area. However, this individual was an excellent communicator with an outstanding attitude, a solid work ethic, and a demonstrated ability to interact with a variety of individuals. In this instance, my intuition told me there was a greater chance of this individual coming up to speed on technical knowledge than of my trying to change the personality and character traits of the other candidates. It was a bit unorthodox, and several people expressed their astonishment at the decision. In hindsight, he was the right choice. The young man got up to speed quickly and to this day enjoys a very successful professional career.

Communication skills are of increasing importance. Is the candidate able to effectively communicate orally and in writing? The ability to communicate to other employees, customers, suppliers, investors, etc., and to convey thoughts and ideas in a way that can be clearly understood are key. If you can't get your point across, nothing will be understood, and nothing will be accomplished.

Adaptability is another essential trait critical in today's ever-changing global environment. The difference between people whose efforts succeed and those whose fail, the successful ones are often the ones who can adapt. Adaptable individuals are versatile. They are resilient. They do not resist change—they accept it, analyze it, and adapt as required. Those who cannot adapt remain entrenched in their routine, clinging to the way things used to be done, falling behind. Often, they will mistakenly blame their company for their own inability to adapt and seek employment elsewhere.

When assessing candidates for your team, you should also assess if the individual would represent the core values and beliefs of the company. Take the time to scour social media, and check out the individual's digital footprint, as their views and comments in social media will carry over to the workplace. An individual who has character and integrity will help maintain the highest standards in the workplace. Moreover, when a crisis occurs, this individual will avoid the negative rhetoric, accept the challenge, and do the right thing. If this individual will be required to operate externally and interact with customers, investors, and suppliers, assess whether this individual would be a good ambassador. If you have any doubts, move on to someone else, as it is easier to develop skills than it is to change someone's character.

The term "team" is used often. Teams are used across the spectrum, whether in business, research, the military, etc. Teams can be formed at any time, in any situation, and for different purposes based on the needs of the company or entity and the task at hand. Teams can be permanent or temporary in nature and comprise these five types:

Types of Teams

1. *Management Team:* This is a traditional, permanent team, made up of the leadership of a company or organization. These individuals meet on a regular basis to review and agree on strategies and issues affecting the organization or industry. The most senior is usually in charge and may delegate leadership on specific issues to other members of the team.

2. *Functional Team:* This is another traditionally formed team, usually permanent in nature, and is an integral part of any organization. This working team is vertically aligned, comprising individuals with similar skill sets functioning in the same department or area, such as marketing, service, or finance. These teams are task oriented, with clearly defined goals and responsibilities. The team leader needs to be confident and capable enough to manage and keep the team on point.

3. *Multifunctional Teams:* This is a commonly used concept in which a team consists of members with various skill sets and proven expertise from across the company or organization. These teams are not always permanent in nature and are often brought together at the request of management to address an issue or opportunity affecting the entire organization, hence the need to cut

across departmental lines. The high-caliber members of a cross-functional team will offer diverse points of view, generating creativity and innovation. One of the most critical elements in the success of the team is a strong team leader, with the requisite interpersonal skills to handle the egos and conflicting views characteristic of such an endeavor.

4. *Task Force:* This is a team formed in response to a problem, an event, or even an opportunity, which must be resolved within a defined period of time, after which the team is disbanded. The members of the team will be from various departments, with selection based on ability to contribute toward resolving the issue. The team requires a strong leader who is empowered to make decisions and take action, since time is of the essence.

5. *Virtual Team:* This is a nontraditional team that is becoming more widely used. These cyber-teams are made possible by technology, facilitating communication and cutting across borders and time zones. These teams work on a common objective, take collective responsibility, and have a great deal of autonomy. There is usually a kick-off meeting conducted via teleconference that describes the objective or assigned tasks, upon which individuals work independently. These individuals are usually allocated a budget under which to operate, using their discretion. Communication takes place via email, phone calls, or teleconferences, and can be highly interactive, depending on the task at hand. These teams

can be highly advantageous, permitting a company to tap into a breadth and depth of expertise not resident within its organization.

However, these types of arrangements do not come without challenges. When forming teams, the individuals chosen should be self-starters, with initiative, a strong work ethic, and a proven track record. These teams are sometimes referred to as "self-managed teams," however, it is inadvisable not to have a leader, as someone needs to coordinate, provide guidance, and track progress. The leader of this team needs to be an excellent communicator, as this team will include a broad array of personnel, potentially from different cultural and linguistic backgrounds, which can be a barrier to communication if not skillfully handled.

There are a number of aspects to consider when building an effective team. In order for talent to be harnessed and synergy to be generated, there are attributes that must be resident among the members. These attributes apply to any team, situation, or environment. When putting a team together, keep the following ten characteristics in mind:

Characteristics of a Good Team

1. *Chemistry:* The most important factor in the success of a team is the chemistry between its members. You can have a team loaded with talent, but if they cannot work well and relate with each other, performance will

be compromised, never reaching its full potential—especially if the team will be together for an extended period. Teams with good chemistry understand the different qualities of each member and what each individual contributes. They work together, maximize their strengths, and minimize their weaknesses, harboring respect for each other and understanding that each person approaches problems differently. The sum total of these interactions determines success.

2. *Diversity:* Team members should be selected based on their talent, skill sets, and contribution to the mission. Each member should contribute a unique skill and competence, complementing and balancing the strengths and weaknesses of other team members. You do not want a group of like-minded individuals, as this will encourage groupthink, which inhibits the open exchange of ideas and thwarts creativity. You cannot have a team comprising mostly Type A personalities, who are hard chargers or drivers. Conversely, you cannot have a team consisting mostly of individuals who are so diplomatic they spend more time trying to gain consensus and avoiding conflicts of opinion. This will stifle innovation and lead to groupthink, and, consequently, there won't be any bold or out-of-the-box solutions emanating from this group.

3. *Resources:* The team should have the collective human resources required to complete the various tasks. In addition, the team should be provided with sources of

information, reports, data, budget (if needed), and the necessary decision-making authority to achieve their goals.

4. *Right Size:* The size of the team depends on the scope, the complexity of the tasks, and the amount of time available. Having too many team members is unwieldy, can lead to misunderstandings or confusion, and risks an overlap of roles and responsibilities. Conversely, too few team members can thwart the purpose of the team, as the range of expertise and discourse will be limited.

5. *Clarity:* There should be a clear understanding of the goals, objectives, metrics, and timelines, with an agreed-upon plan on how to attain them. Every team member's role and responsibility should be defined and understood. You do not want team members working at cross-purposes or on redundant tasks, creating conflict later.

6. *Communication:* Team members should communicate openly and honestly with each other. They should not be hesitant to express their views and opinions, even if they are critical of others, as full transparency involves the ability to express and receive constructive criticism. Team members must keep each other apprised of their progress, with information viewed as something to be shared instead of parceled out. Members should be attentive, effective listeners, receptive to input from other team members.

7. *Attitude:* Team members should have a positive and enthusiastic attitude regarding their tasks and the prospects for success. They should be willing participants, cooperating freely with other team members, and should view this as a collaborative effort, rather than competitive. Motivated and with a can-do attitude, they understand that, when the team wins, everyone wins.

8. *Leadership:* Leadership and team effectiveness go hand in hand. In order for a team to be effective, it needs a strong leader, and in order for a leader to be effective, a good team is needed. The leader manages the personalities involved, promoting both cohesiveness and constructive debate. The leader provides direction and encouragement, facilitates collaboration, and ensures open and honest communication among the team, with each person respecting the views of the others, ensuring that meetings are productive and consequent. Special attention is paid to team-busting behavior, with the leader making whatever personnel adjustments are necessary in the best interests of the team and the tasks at hand. The leader does not overlook the importance of teambuilding, including activities that foster the team's ability to relate to and understand each other.

9. *Trust:* There must be mutual trust among the team members. Each team member knows he or she can rely on every other team member. Everyone understands their role and contributes, sharing the load and not working

in isolation. Team members are empowered to perform, trusting that each team member will say what they do and do what they say.

10. *Respect:* There must be mutual respect, professionally and personally. Knowing that teamwork requires decisions, the views of each team member should be considered and acknowledged. A dissenting opinion or disagreement must be heard and respected, versus criticized, keeping it professional, not personal. Conflicts should be effectively resolved, with the team leader intervening as required. Once a decision is made, even if it is not unanimous, the entire team moves forward in lockstep and unity, with a clearly defined purpose and sense of commitment.

Forming a team does not guarantee teamwork; you have to work at it. The characteristics of teams that fail are the converse of teams that succeed. The primary reason a team is not successful is almost always people-related—a lack of team chemistry, resulting in poor dynamics, a lack of leadership, or a lack of communication. Those leading or forming a team should continually bear in mind that a team is a dynamic and complicated system—it is ever changing and can be affected by both internal and external factors. As a leader, pay close attention to the chemistry and dynamics of the team. Take every opportunity to organize events so they can interact, always keep the best interests and purpose of the team front and center, and ensure open communication, information exchange, and clarity of purpose.

When bringing someone on board or forming a team, the selection of the individual should be based on the needs of the organization and the tasks required to attain its goals. A chain is only as strong as its weakest link, thus, when forming a team and evaluating candidates, keep the following criteria in mind:

1. *Competence:* Does the individual have the requisite skills and acumen required, and can this be validated?

2. *Chemistry:* Does the individual have the emotional quotient required for effective team dynamics and communication?

3. *Character:* Will the individual represent the best interests of the team and organization, engendering trust and respect?

4. *Clarity:* Is there an understanding of the goals and objectives, with each team member's role clearly defined?

5. *Leadership:* Is there leadership in place to manage the team?

CHAPTER FOUR

Fundamentals

"Success doesn't come from what you do occasionally—
it comes from what you do consistently."

Success or failure in whatever endeavor or field you pursue is determined by adhering to and improving on the fundamentals or the basics. There are always new and different programs rolled out, oftentimes with catchy terminology, but it is simply a repackaging or embellishment of the basic prerequisites essential for any individual or organization to be successful. If you acknowledge and master the basics, you can build on them and better adapt to the world around you. You will successfully overcome the challenges you'll face and take advantage of the opportunities that arise. If you never master the basics, you'll never master yourself, and you'll be destined for mediocrity.

People and organizations often lose sight of the basics. Fundamental work can be drudgery—it is boring, repetitive, and hard work. It doesn't present well or make for good theater. However, personal or organizational success is achieved only by properly executing and improving on fundamental processes over a sustained period of time. Conversely, failure is the inability to properly execute the processes over a period of time, with the accumulation of bad practices resulting in errors and lost opportunities. It is not uncommon for this latter scenario to occur in larger organizations, when attention to quantitative measures results in a lack of attention to the core quality aspects of the business. For example, compromises made on training and personnel development will ultimately have a ripple effect across the organization.

The most direct route to achieving excellence is paying attention to and properly executing the fundamentals. Many new businesses fail because of their inability to apply the fundamentals—the foundation of their day-to-day operations—to their unique business strategy or concept. This is often due to bad choices when assembling the team; some members may not have the skill sets necessary to delve into the inner workings of the business, or may not appreciate the importance of mastering the fundamentals. They spend more time on strategy or putting together focus groups when they should be devoting their time to becoming the best at what they do day to day, week to week, month to month, and year after year.

Focusing on the fundamentals is a common thread for many successful coaches in sports. Phil Jackson, Vince Lombardi, and Bill Belichick are examples of coaches with an obsession for details and mastering the fundamentals. They realized the margin of success or failure is based on consistently executing the fundamentals. The accumulation of small improvements over a sustained period of time ultimately translates to gains in performance and productivity, yielding significant results and progress toward goals.

The core factors of success have been covered in previous chapters. The rest of this chapter will focus on the ten fundamentals essential for you to become successful, be fulfilled, and realize your full potential. Of these ten, the first is the most important, but each of these must be resident within you as they build on each other. The combination of all ten is powerful, and the absence of even a few of them will endanger your ability to unleash your true potential. Keep these in mind at all times, and work on them continuously—the results will follow.

Ten Fundamentals for Personal Success

1. *Self-confidence:* Your success in your endeavors will largely depend upon the confidence you have in yourself. You may fail from time to time, but if you are strong and resolute, you will never be defeated. Your conviction and strong self-belief will carry you through. This sense of self-worth must come from within, not by comparing yourself with others. You must be true to yourself and never betray your values. There will be adversity and failure—you may lose a job or lose money, but you must never lose the most valuable asset, which is the belief you have in yourself and your ability. No one can take this away from you; it can be taken from you only by you. How you see yourself is how others perceive you.

Your confidence and can-do attitude are contagious and have an accelerating effect. Conversely, self-doubt and low self-esteem have a decelerating effect, limiting the opportunities you pursue and that are available to you. No one wants to work with someone riddled with self-doubt. You must find the strength and willpower to reach your full potential by making the decision to invest in yourself and commit to doing whatever it takes. It is there—you just have to tap into it, develop it, and make it happen.

2. *Habits:* These are the small things you do every day, the array of daily decisions and processes that establish your flow or rhythm. These habits pertain to both your personal and professional life. They contribute to nearly half of your behavior each day and serve to define you and how you operate. Some of these habits are formed during childhood, and others are formed through a variety of influences, such as education, sports, military service, and peers you spend time with. The sum of your habits shapes you into the person you are and sets the pattern for your life. Good habits develop you into an efficient and effective individual, improving your productivity. Bad habits result in personal inefficiency, wasted time, slipshod work, and subpar results in all aspects of your life. Consequently, there is nothing more important you can do than develop a set of habits that make you the most efficient and effective person possible, setting the stage for your success.

This topic could be the subject of an entire chapter, or even a book for that matter. It covers myriad topics, some of them as seemingly mundane as to-do lists, but it is ultimately up to you to develop a set of habits or routine that works best for you. You are more likely to follow through with something if you develop a plan, become accountable to yourself, and stick to it. After a while, this routine, which could also be called "practice," reinforces your behavior and becomes a good habit, empowering you to take the next step. Then, you move on to another habit, one step at a time, one good habit at a time, tackling the areas you need to develop to improve performance and personal efficiency.

3. *Skill:* We live in a world where specialization is the maxim. If you want to stand out at what you do, you have to be good—in fact, be your *best*—and master all aspects. Even before that, as alluded to in an earlier chapter, it is imperative that you find a professional field that is a good fit for you. It should be one that aligns with your interests and beliefs, and one for which you have the personality and talent to be successful. Passion without talent and skill is a nonstarter; talent and skill without passion means you are merely going through the motions. Neither combination is a winning formula. While you may have a natural proclivity that enables you to get the job done, to reach your full potential, you must be well versed and highly trained in all facets of your work. The more you know about your work, the

more you are seen as an expert, and the more efficient, effective, confident, and accomplished you will be. You will stand out as someone who consistently does the right things in the right way. If you want to realize your true potential, you must unleash it, and that happens only through training, dedication, and commitment. This is easier said than done, and it is what holds many people back. True ability is hampered by lack of preparation and unwillingness to put in the time to become an expert. Whatever field you are in will require basic skills that must be developed and honed to perfection if you want to realize your full potential. Whether it be tech, finance, media, sports, or any other field of endeavor, you must not only be willing but also have the courage and conviction to master the critical skills required to be successful.

4. *Discipline:* Self-discipline is mandatory; it is the engine that powers your journey to whatever you want to accomplish. Discipline gives you the will to take the necessary actions to improve yourself, the courage to leave your comfort zone and face your fears, and the self-control to stick to a regimen. Without discipline, you will not face challenges that need to be confronted, and, as a result, you will miss opportunities. You will become stagnant, spend more time on leisure activities and whatever is most comfortable, going nowhere. Success usually requires committing to do the tough, sometimes unpleasant, things necessary for you to grow

and succeed, and delaying or putting off those things that you find gratifying but do not help you grow.

The lure of instant gratification is one of the obstacles you will face along the path to success. Delaying gratification is a trait common to all successful people, who realize that sacrifices must be made for their own good. Regardless of what you may think, we are not born with or without discipline; it is a learned behavior. Rather than make discipline your obstacle, make it your strength. Define what you want to do, develop a plan with goals, develop a routine, make the commitment to follow through, hold yourself accountable, and dump the excuses. Over time, this regimen results in your new approach becoming ingrained. Small successes mount up, bad habits are abandoned, good habits are developed, and you are in control. As someone once told me, "Discipline is not something you do *to* someone; it is something you do *for* someone." Do this for yourself.

5. *Initiative:* The limitations you face are often those you place upon yourself. When you want something to happen, you must commit, with the courage and self-motivation to see it through. Hoping things will work out is not a strategy; you have to *make* things work out. You are the master of your own destiny; you can do great things, but *only you* can do it. One hallmark of successful people is that they are proactive, and they take it upon themselves to do the things that are necessary to attain their goals, undeterred by the naysayers. Their

success is not sudden or serendipitous. It is a deliberate series of small steps, all of which build upon each other.

Successful people are not mildly interested—they are personally committed. They take the initiative, they never stop learning, and they maintain momentum. You, too, must take the initiative and the steps necessary to attain your goals. There will be success and failure, perhaps in equal measures, but this journey of self-discovery will enable you to uncover the hidden capabilities lying within you, bolstering your sense of direction. These experiences will mold you into the person you are destined to be as you explore your interests, discover more about yourself, and unleash your potential. However, that first step must be taken, so take it. Then take the next step, and another after that, moving forward with courage, confidence, and commitment.

6. *Adaptability:* If you like how things are going now, appreciate them, for this will surely change. As Charles Darwin stated, "It is not the strongest of the species that survive, nor the most intelligent, but the ones most responsive to change." The same tenet holds true in your life, as your ability to adapt to changing circumstances is central to your success. Do not confuse adapting with coping, as there is a distinct difference. The challenge for you is not only to survive but to thrive, by having the situational awareness to understand what is going on and to react accordingly.

When someone is in a position for a sustained period of time, it is not unusual for that person to become accustomed to the status quo, settling into a stagnant routine, never leaving their comfort zone. Know this: if you keep doing the same things you always have, while ignoring what is going on around you, failure will eventually come knocking on your door. Successful people and organizations understand this and are always willing to look at new and different ways of doing things. They are eager to receive feedback and to challenge the status quo, and are not so focused on Plan A that they are unwilling to consider Plan B or C. As you begin to pursue your career, understand that you will frequently deal with change or unexpected demands. Rather than fight this change, be flexible, be open to different points of view, and always be ready to adapt—the world will not wait for you.

7. *Integrity:* People do business with companies that deliver what they promise, stand behind their work, and accept accountability. These companies have integrity and a good reputation. Just like a company, your integrity follows you wherever you go and ultimately becomes your reputation. The term "integrity" is bandied about quite a bit in the business world. My definition of a person with "integrity" is someone whose character is beyond reproach and who always conducts himself or herself in an ethical and respectful manner, with a high degree of transparency.

Self-interest is the antithesis of integrity, as individuals with integrity seek a higher purpose than themselves. Honesty and accountability are central, both of which engender trust and loyalty. People gravitate toward individuals with integrity because they are trustworthy and dependable. Their actions match their words, and they accept accountability for their actions. Individuals with integrity do not take shortcuts or make compromises based on self-interest, which erodes their integrity. You can be highly qualified, with the best education and the best training, but if you lack integrity, you compromise your chances and set a pattern that will ultimately catch up with you. Always be a person of integrity.

8. *Demeanor:* The quality of your work and the way you are perceived are affected by your conduct. A positive attitude, a pleasant disposition, being prompt, thorough, courteous, and kind, with an unshakeable belief in what you are doing, all generate enthusiasm within you and radiate to others. When people meet someone with these traits—one who displays confidence, stands tall, looks them in the eye, and has a firm handshake—the first impression will be favorable and lasting. You must remain undeterred by the obstacles in your path, even the failures, and not let them weaken your resolve, commitment, or enthusiasm. A lack of enthusiasm is noticeable to all around you and does not imbue confidence. Your enthusiasm is generated by your actions and your beliefs, not by the money you make or the position you hold.

Money and position are extrinsic, and while important, it is your intrinsic components that determine progress in these other areas. Having the proper demeanor and right attitude will enable you to deal with those inconvenient and unpleasant situations you'll face with courage and an even-tempered disposition.

At all times, strive to maintain self-control and avoid overreaction, regardless of circumstances. A lack of self-control results in overemotional responses, and when you lose control of your emotions, you lose control of your mind and make bad decisions, undermining your performance and your perception. Be seen as a person who is in control and has their act together, avoiding drama and theatrics. All of this exudes an aura of success that will resonate with those around you, especially in times of crisis, which is when you will shine. With the right attitude and demeanor, you can remain unfazed in the face of adversity and failure, and you will accomplish your goals.

9. *Balance:* This often-overlooked item may seem a bit out of place. However, it is important not only in theory but also in practice. Your greatest asset is you, which includes your mind, your body, and your spirit. If you have too much time and effort invested in one area at the expense of others, it is a hindrance; it will throw you off balance, as each one plays off the other. Mental activity keeps you sharp, prolongs your effectiveness, and improves your health. The same holds true for your physical body, as

exercise increases your efficiency, contributes to your health, and enhances your mental performance. And just as you have interest in work, you have interests elsewhere which should not be ignored—or likewise, vigorously pursued at the expense of other areas.

When I worked at the North American corporate office of a large West German company, I reported to the president of the company. On weekends, one of my routines was to take my young son to the corporate office so he could see the fish tank in the president's office. It was a large tank housing a great number of fish, and my son very much enjoyed watching them. This became such a routine that the president would even leave a note to the effect of, "Mr. Stuvek can bring his son in to see the fish tank any time he wants." During these weekend excursions, I came to notice that every time we visited, there was a division manager in his office, regardless of which day we showed up. I would always greet him and let him get back to whatever he was doing.

Several months later, there was an opening for a very senior management position. Everyone expected that the division manager who spent all those weekend days in the office was a lock for the position, but to everyone's surprise, the president announced the position was going to someone else. The rejected candidate was aghast and objected with, "I don't understand why I wasn't selected." The president turned to him and said, "You are in your office seven days a week. You cannot effectively plan

your work; you don't know how to delegate, and you
have no balance. I don't need a burn-out on my staff." I
have always remembered that conversation and harkened
back to my time at the Naval Academy, when one of the
mission statements was "development of mind, body, and
spirit." In this respect, pay attention to all three, none
at the expense of the other. You will be glad you did.

10. *Decision-making:* You can have all of the fundamental
qualities listed above, but if you do not make good
decisions, it is all for naught. No matter how smart
you are or how much training you have, you will never
reach your full potential if you make bad decisions.
Someone can be extremely qualified, with outstanding
credentials, yet still have a mundane and disappointing
track record. How? It comes down to three inextricably
linked factors—fear, caution, and lack of confidence.
As mentioned earlier, you must face your fears and get
out of your comfort zone. Just because you are in a
good position and making great money doesn't mean
you are better off in that position long-term. It may be
easy to rationalize staying put, and at the time, it may
make perfect sense to you. You'll remain cautious and
wait for the right opportunity, when things are lined up
perfectly. But the longer you wait, the less inclined you
are to do anything, and you slowly convince yourself
there is no reason to change. However, by not taking a
chance—call it a *risk*—you stand to lose more over the
long term by not risking something *now*.

You have to constantly challenge yourself if you want to grow and keep moving forward, avoiding stagnancy and complacency. You also have to ensure you have all the facts before making a decision, recognizing there are always instances when snap decisions are required based on circumstances. In those instances, trust your intuition, and go for it. If you do not have urgent time constraints, seek the truth and get the facts.

Going back to my time with the West German company, when I first moved to the Corporate Office, I was initially reporting to one of the vice presidents. One of the first things he said to me was, "Stuvek, I know you are one of those Naval Academy types who prides himself on being decisive and in charge. However, remember this business is something that develops over a period of time. It involves millions of dollars, it takes months to get the order, and there are numerous decision-makers. It then takes months to produce the equipment, and then it has to be shipped and installed, which takes several weeks. There are a lot of moving parts. Don't screw things up by jumping in and making a decision if you don't have all of the facts."

This was good advice for any situation, assuming there are no time constraints. When making decisions, remember that it is both an art and a science. Do not make decisions out of fear; get the facts so that you understand the problem and are able to make an informed and objective decision. If you can't get all the facts or are prohibited by a time constraint, trust your instinct.

As you go forward on your journey of self-development, self-discovery, and self-fulfillment, remember to:

1. *Act:* Execute in accordance with these ten fundamentals; if your fundamentals are solid, you are solid.

2. *Train and Prepare:* Build a strong foundation, and create opportunities.

3. *Conquer:* Overcome fear, caution, and self-doubt.

4. *Risk:* Be willing to take calculated risks; continue to move forward.

5. *Decisions:* Make good decisions, in the right way, for the right reasons.

Future

"The best way to predict the future is to create it."

You have finished the book. You have a lot to digest and much to do. As you now understand, it is not one thing, but a number of issues that must be considered and, when acted upon, will determine what you ultimately do in life and how well you do it. Which brings me to the primary goal of this book—to provide a step-by-step guide for your personal and professional development in a sequential, concise, and clear manner, so that you can take your fate into your hands and create your future. It is eminently doable if you follow the advice contained herein.

What happens after this is entirely up to you. The difference between who you are and who you want to be is determined by what you *do*. Life has no remote—you have to get up and change it yourself. However, if you are not willing to take control, nothing will change. You cannot wait for someone or some set of fortuitous circumstances to shape your life. It's on you.

I urge you to start now. Do not procrastinate, as "later" often leads to "never." Put yourself in an action mode; make a decision, take that first step, and then another. Remember that success doesn't come from what you do occasionally—it comes from what you do consistently. Each step builds on the previous step, with your confidence and belief increasing incrementally. All of this adds up, like compounded interest. It will take time and won't always be easy, but ultimately you will get there. Later, you will look back and be glad you made the effort.

I wish you all the best.

About the Author

Fred Stuvek Jr. has achieved extraordinary success in diverse realms. Born in West Virginia and raised in Pennsylvania, he has been inducted into the Pennsylvania Sports Hall of Fame for achievements in football, basketball, baseball, and track. He graduated from the United States Naval Academy, after lettering three years as quarterback for the Midshipmen. After service as a Naval Officer, he transitioned to the business world where he has held senior leadership positions in private and public companies, both domestically and internationally. Key successes include an international medical imaging start-up that led to a successful IPO, and forming a private medical services company, which he subsequently sold. His first book, *It Starts With You: Turn Your Goals Into Success,* quickly became an international bestseller, garnering praise for its no nonsense approach to going after what you want out of life. From the playing field, to the war room, to the board room his leadership and accomplishments have given him a distinct perspective and a results-oriented mindset. To learn more about Fred and his work, please visit www.fredstuvek.com.

Made in the USA
Monee, IL
03 July 2020

35558576R00105